Puzzle Projects
for Woodworkers

Puzzle Projects
for Woodworkers

Allan J. Boardman

Linden Publishing Inc.
Fresno, California

Puzzle Projects for Woodworkers

Text © 2007 Allan Boardman
Photos © 2007 Linden Publishing
Line Art © 2007 Linden Publishing

ISBN: 978-1-933502-11-3

135798642
Printed in Thailand

Library of Congress Cataloging-in-Publication Data
Boardman, Allan J., 1934-
 Puzzle projects for woodworkers / Allan J. Boardman.
   p. cm.
 Includes bibliographical references.
 ISBN 978-1-933502-11-3 (pbk. : alk. paper)
 1. Wooden toy making. 2. Puzzles. I. Title.
 TT174.5.W6B63 2007
 745.592--dc22

                      2007035905

Linden Publishing Inc.
2006 S. Mary
Fresno CA 93721
www.lindenpub.com
800-345-4447

Dedication

To Lina, who has tolerated my hobbies, habits, idiosyncrasies, collections, and mess for forty-seven years. Truly amazing!

Acknowledgements

My father, who bought me my first puzzle and launched me into a lifelong love affair with both puzzles and woodworking.

All woodworkers and puzzle designers, past and present, who have brought so much richness to my life.

The staff at Linden Publishing, notably David Getts, who made and photographed the puzzles, Jim Goold, who made the drawings, and John Kelsey, who did the book design and layout.

Contents

Bi-Burr page 14

Please Drop In page 32

Pocoloco page 16

Lateral Thinking page 36

MMMM page 26

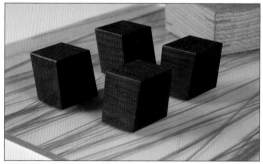

Blockhead page 42

Aha Box   page 48

Pandora's Box   page 74

Nob's Neverending Puzzle   page 55

Pegasus   page 78

Fifth Avenue   page 62

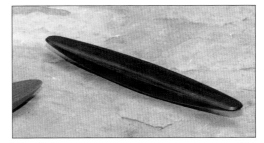

The Celt   page 84

Level 5 Notchable
Six-Piece Burr   page 68

Fritz the Wonder Dog   page 89

Puzzle Projects for Woodworkers   **7**

Preface

Why spend workshop time making mechanical puzzles? They certainly aren't the most useful of objects and many people do not even like to play with them. If you really want a clever puzzle, a little shopping will surely turn one up. But utility is seldom the only reason a woodworker picks a particular project. There is the joy of making something with your own hands, using your favorite wood, adding a personal feature to an existing design, and building to higher standards than are commercially common, not to mention justifying all those tools you simply couldn't live without. Beyond all of these valid reasons, puzzles are excellent for honing shop skills with a minimum investment in time and materials, and they hold the potential of providing amusement and challenge for those on your gift list that actually enjoy playing with them.

Many books about puzzles have appeared in the last hundred years, but the majority of these have been aimed at puzzle enthusiasts, not serious woodworkers. This book attempts to bring both camps together in the hope of making woodworkers into puzzlers and vice versa. The two fields of interest, each with a long and interesting history, form a natural marriage. Amateur woodworkers are constantly solving puzzles in their shops—how shall I design this jig, in what order shall I proceed through this project, how can I possibly fit all this stuff into my garage. And puzzlers, if they were to develop

the capability and skills, will find that they could add many new and wonderful designs to their collections by making them in their own shop.

Contemporary designers created nearly all the puzzles selected for this compendium. Most have never been produced commercially—if you want one of these, you will simply have to make it. These designs collectively challenge the woodworker to do his or her best. As brainteasers, they vary in difficulty from rather easy to quite challenging, but all will give anyone who finds their solutions a feeling of satisfaction. So, tune up your tools, grab a few off-cuts lying about your shop, and begin. The rewards are really worth it!

Introduction

Woodworkers serious about their craft seldom run out of things to make. And between projects there is always plenty to do in the shop—maintaining tools, rearranging equipment to make more room or improve efficiency, sharpening, cleaning up, and so forth. These brief interludes between major works are also times for small projects. Mechanical puzzles are wonderful gap fillers because they are often challenging to make in their own right, the finished puzzles provide amusement, and making them can enhance skills needed in projects that are more complex.

No doubt many of these puzzles can be made quickly and crudely and still be fun to play with and solve. But instead, think of making them as learning experiences, practice exercises that will find applicability in a broad range of larger undertakings in your workshop. Many of the projects you will encounter in the following pages incorporate joinery, techniques, and challenges common in cabinetry and furniture making.

If you select an unsuitable piece of wood for a project, humidity changes may later render the parts too tight to fit together, too loose to stay assembled, or may even cause a glue joint to fail. You simply cannot afford to ignore wood's response to humidity when doing careful work. If you are too impatient to make an accurate jig, parts that should be identical won't be. If you ignore the need to properly set up your table saw or planer, the surface quality and dimensions

you need will just not be achieved. Sandpaper, while it might improve the way a surface feels, will alter the dimensions you are after, possibly ruining the project. If you do things in the wrong order, you may later wish you had thought the process through more carefully. Learning such skills, sorting out issues like accuracy, precision, and work standards, and acquiring this kind of experience, is far more cost and time effective when the project is a puzzle rather than, say, a desk or grandfather clock.

In addition to skill, experience, diligence and the like, care and precision in woodworking requires adopting a certain state of mind. "Good enough" is seldom good enough. You have to establish in your mind's eye what your criterion is for exactness, project by project, detail by detail. Sometimes it is the way two parts fit together for a sliding, no slop, fit. Sometimes it is the tightness of a glue joint—wood to wood, zero width glue line. As you prepare the parts of any multi-piece project, initial cutting is determined by the design dimensions, but the final jig stop adjustments or clean up operations are often dictated by the required fit. Working tolerances are mostly comfortable and easy to obtain with ordinary care, but on occasion, precision to within one or two thousandths of an inch (much less than the thickness of a piece of paper), is critical to the workings of the puzzle. Although most woodworkers do not normally think in terms of thousandths of an inch, the most skillfully crafted wooden objects usually reflect the application of precise standards. A ruler or a protractor is useful for the initial cutting, but offering up one part to another for a test fit, or dry assembly, often determines if you are "on the mark."

Accuracy and precision are not the same thing, and although most of us are a little loose in using such terms, they really have different—usefully different—meanings. Consider the cubical elements of the *Fifth Avenue* puzzle. The plan calls for ¾-inch cubes, but no one would notice or care if they measured, say, 1 inch on a side, although one could say that would be a whopping inaccuracy. It would still be a great puzzle and such a dimensional or scale change would not, by itself, detract from how well made it was. However, if the cubes differed from each other by even 1/32 inch, or if their sides were not truly square, the sloppiness and lack of precision would label the puzzle as poorly made. In the same way, a flush drawer in a desk, called out on a plan as 15 inches wide, could be made a bit smaller or larger without any problem at all, just as long as it fits precisely in its opening, with a small and uniform space around it.* (For those woodworkers accustomed to using metric measurements, please see page 94.)

As you leaf through these pages, try to discern what there is about each project that makes it a puzzle and what about the design is purely decorative or even arbitrary. A trick box sometimes relies on the selection of specific corner joints to hide the opening gimmick. Other times, the corner joint has nothing to do with the puzzle and is only selected because the designer or woodworker wanted to employ one method or another. If a tray is part of the project, perhaps a sliding block puzzle or packing puzzle, the

bottom of the tray might be set into a rabbeted frame, or into grooves, or even butt glued to the bottom of the frame—your choice. Feel free to interchange these features from one project to another—just so long as you do not adversely affect the function of the puzzles. Chamfer or ease edges to give the puzzle parts a friendly feel—after all, these objects are meant to be played with. But be careful to do this detail work after you are assured that critical dimensions will not be disturbed and that no unintended clue to the solution will be given. Waiting until the entire project is assembled before easing edges may not always be the most efficient procedure, but it is often the surest and safest.

For some projects, the properties of the wood you choose are more important than in other projects, but in general, any attractive, readily available species will do, be it hardwood or softwood, (though hardwood is often preferred because of its beauty and durability). However, care must be taken that the stock you are working with is dry and has been sitting around your shop for some months so that it is relatively dimensionally stable. Some species work better than others do, of course. Some are prone to burn on the table saw—a sharp blade and well-tuned saw are musts. Others are too soft to hold up well when the children or grandchildren (or you) toss the puzzle pieces around the room in frustration. Dense exotics, though beautiful, are often not the best choices for puzzle making. Sometimes because of their natural oiliness they do not glue well, sometimes they are difficult to work with hand tools, and often their hardness becomes a problem when trying to obtain that perfect "light friction" fit of two sliding parts. But to be a woodworker is to learn—in time you will have your favorites if you don't already.

---

*The difference between accuracy and precision came under the spotlight in the latter half of the 18th century when John Harrison, a British clockmaker, attempted to win the £20,000 prize established by Parliament for solving the longitude problem—determining longitude at sea to improve marine navigation. He designed and built a chronometer that worked well, but on its trial voyage, it proved to be off a few seconds a day, more than allowed by the conditions for winning the prize. Though the clock was slightly inaccurate, it was off the same amount every day, proving its precision. Eventually, Parliament recognized that minor calibration would cancel the small inaccuracy and awarded Harrison the prize.

The tools needed for these projects are those one would find in any modestly equipped woodshop. It is essential that you have a very accurate means of setting up and checking parts, tools, and jigs for squareness and straightness—a bargain-table square will not do. You will be wise not to begin any of these projects until all the tools in your shop have been carefully adjusted and tuned. Many of the illustrations and photographs presented show the use of one tool or method. Obviously, there are other choices; you will have to adapt the construction suggestions to your tools and experience. Ninety-degree and forty-five degree stops on your machines must be spot on. Edge tools must be in excellent working order and sharp. Be sure there is plenty of light over your workbench. If you are already proficient with their use, most of these projects can be completed using only hand tools. Or, if you are serious about learning these traditional techniques, making puzzles will help you with this quest.

As required, jigs should be made with adjustable stops for precision tweaking of parts that must fit just so. A machine screw threaded through a block of wood glued to the jig or clamped to the saw table can serve as a micro-adjustable stop. Always prepare enough stock to allow for some trial and error in your set-ups, or even that unintended "whoops."

Scan through all the projects before selecting one to start with. Some of the tips and techniques given in one chapter, or in the four technical notes, may have applicability to other projects. Follow the construction details, photos, and illustrations presented for each project to the extent that this is useful. There are a minimum of step-by-step or detailed instructions; the text accompanying each project is mainly intended to highlight and emphasize the more demanding aspects of each puzzle and offer some guidance on at least one way of approaching the construction. For optimum learning and fun, experiment a little. Step outside the instructions and try your own methods. You will know by playing with the final product if you have done

it right, and if you haven't, well, simply study the results, identify your errors, devise better methods, and start again, benefiting from the experience. If you make a second or third attempt, it would be quite unusual if the subsequent products didn't get better and better.

The projects are not presented in any particular order, such as increasing construction difficulty or increasing puzzle solution difficulty, since perceived difficulty and actual difficulty can vary quite a bit. Simple parts requiring great precision can be harder to make than more complex pieces with looser tolerances. Actual difficulty and the amount of time required to make each puzzle will depend not only on the intrinsic nature of the design, but on the maker's experience and skill level, the methods used, plus the tools and equipment at hand. And the challenge one faces in attempting to solve a particular puzzle depends a great deal on how the individual's brain works.

Almost any finish is acceptable for puzzles, but care must be taken not to inadvertently alter the fit of mating parts by using a finish with significant build-up. Danish oil works well in most cases, offering some degree of protection from soil and enhancing the appearance of the wood without any danger of changing the dimensions or creating any unwanted stickiness.

Caution! Making puzzles means working with small parts. In addition to all the other important safety rules—protect your eyes, lungs, ears, and extremities—that have been drummed into your head, you must devise jigs to accurately position small parts for cutting without getting your hands too close to saw blades. You will get better parts and preserve your fingers for future projects! It will often be necessary to work at a table saw with the blade guard removed. This must be a red flag requiring an extra measure of caution.

—*Allan Boardman, August 2007*

Figure 1—Bi-Burr by Nob Yoshigahara

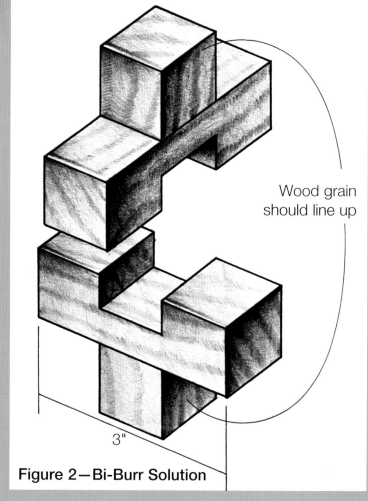

Wood grain
should line up

3"

Figure 2—Bi-Burr Solution

Chapter 1

Bi-Burr

Designed by Nob Yoshigahara

To a woodworker, the *Bi-Burr*, **Figure 1** and **Figure 2**, is nothing more than a simple lap, or bridle, joint with two extra pieces added. But to a puzzle enthusiast, in its assembled form it looks like a familiar three-piece burr. Burr puzzles are generally made of three, six, or more sticks, usually square in cross section. The sticks are notched in a variety of ways, depending on the design, so that they can be assembled into a symmetrical, three dimensional object that can be disassembled and reassembled with some degree of challenge.

What makes the *Bi-Burr* different is that, while it looks like an ordinary three-piece burr, it really consists of only two separate, and in this case identical, pieces, as shown in **Figure 2**. An experienced puzzler will try pushing, pulling, or twisting all three sticks in turn, looking for the key piece—there is none. If well made, even a close examination of the center joint will not reveal how the puzzle comes apart. But making it well is the real challenge. Were this a simple lap joint in a piece of furniture, glue would be used to hold it together permanently. But since the *Bi-Burr* is intended to be taken apart and put

Nob Yoshigahara (1936-2004)

Puzzlemaster, genius, International Ambassador of Puzzles, legend, and one of the best puzzle inventors the world has ever known, are some of the terms that have been used to describe Nob. His enormous accomplishments encompass inventing and designing about two hundred mechanical puzzles that were produced commercially, with at least eight million sold in Japan and America. Rush Hour, made and sold by ThinkFun, is one of the most popular puzzles of all time. It has received fourteen awards from educational and popular publications. Nob also invented or helped to develop other ThinkFun puzzles: Hoppers, Flip-it, Shape-by-Shape, and Lunar Lockout.

Nob designed his first mechanical puzzle in 1955 at age nineteen. Amazingly, his most popular puzzle was the 100 year old classic four-piece "T" Puzzle which he redesigned and to which he added 20 additional problems. It has sold over 4 million copies. — *Jerry Slocum*

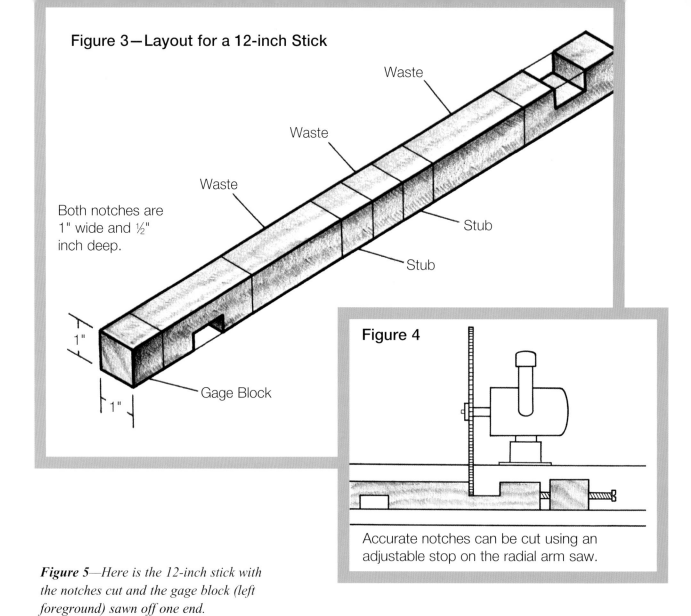

Figure 3—Layout for a 12-inch Stick

Waste

Waste

Waste

Both notches are
1" wide and ½"
inch deep.

Stub

Stub

1"

1"

Gage Block

Figure 4

Accurate notches can be cut using an
adjustable stop on the radial arm saw.

*Figure 5—Here is the 12-inch stick with
the notches cut and the gage block (left
foreground) sawn off one end.*

together repeatedly, only friction holds the two parts together. There must be enough friction so that the parts do not fall apart on their own or even feel loose, yet if they were too tight, disassembly would be too difficult.

It is the nature of wood to swell and shrink in response to changes in humidity, more in width and thickness than in length, so it is important that the piece of wood you are using has been sitting around the shop long enough to have reached a reasonably stable moisture content, and that your shop environment is reasonably similar to your house environment. This requirement generally applies to all well crafted wooden projects, but in the case of this puzzle and several others in this book, it is critical to the success of the project.

Prepare a stick, perhaps 12 inches long (any species of moderate density will do: walnut, cherry, or ash, for example), to a square cross section. One inch on a side is a good size, but it really can be any dimension (**Figure 3**). All four sides of the stick should be planed or jointed so that they are parallel, very uniform, and free of tool marks (see *Making a Square Stick*, page 18). Then cut the ends of the stick to be sure that they are square and clean. Cut off an approximate one-inch length of the stick, to be used later to gage the width of the notches. Set up your table saw or radial arm saw to cut notches half the depth of the thickness of the stick—½ inch in this case.

Although a dado blade can be used, it is just as simple, and probably better for this project, to make multiple passes with a general purpose blade. Using a scrap piece, set up the stop for the first cut 1 inch from the end. Make the first cut in both ends of the puzzle work piece, and work your way along the notch, widening cut by cut, adjusting the stop as you go. When you get close to the full width of the notch, use the gage block and proceed slowly with small adjustments of

Figure 6—*Use the gage block to test the width of the notches.*

the stop position until the gage block fits rather snugly in the notch. Make the last notch cuts in the workpiece with this stop setting (**Figure 4, Figure 5, Figure 6**). The puzzle parts will be eased later for a perfect fit. Reset the depth of the saw blade to cut through the stick and cut off the two notched pieces to length. With a file or chisel, clean off any saw marks at the bottom of the notches.

As an option, a small cavity can be created at the center of the puzzle to receive a ball bearing that will rattle in the assembled puzzle, leading the uninitiated to realize that the object is to be disassembled. If you want to add this feature, drill a ⅜ inch hole ³⁄₁₆ inch deep at the center of the bottom of both notches. A ¼-inch ball bearing or bead can be dropped in later (**Figure 7**).

For maximum effect, the two stubs that will be

Making a Square Stick

Check for square corners using a machinist's square. Hold the stick up to a bright light. If you detect just a crack of light, it shows an out of square condition.

Use a dial, LED, or vernier caliper to check the thickness of the stick. An inexpensive vernier caliper like this is normally accurate within 0.001 inch.

Making a square stick sounds like it might be a rather basic skill requirement for even the most inexperienced woodworker. And indeed, if the corners need only to be somewhat square, the sides sort of smooth, the stick sort of straight, and it should be kind of uniform down the whole length, the job is indeed rather simple. But when the tolerances get really tight, as is the case when making many mechanical puzzles, to say nothing of cabinetry and furniture, the seemingly simple job can get more difficult. Wood wants to distort when stress is relieved as when ripping a strip off a wide board. Saw marks and burns are common. Saw blades are not always exactly square with their tables; jointer fences are not always adjusted perfectly perpendicular to the bed. Chips of wood often get in the way of precision machining. Then there are snipes at the ends of pieces that have been run through thickness planers. Minimizing these things requires very careful tool adjustments and maintenance

using precision measuring devices and vigilant shop practices—and even so they still happen. Correcting errors or smoothing the sides after cutting can make the situation worse—like the barber evening up sideburns. Making a precise square stick is no simple job.

Even checking for squareness and uniformity requires the right tools and some practice. In making puzzles, it seldom matters if a stick nominally dimensioned at 1 inch on a side is a little over or a little under. Adjusting other dimensions as needed can compensate for such errors. But it nearly always matters that all the sides are the same width from one end to the other, and that the corners are exactly 90 degrees. Even though it might be somewhat embarrassing for you to spend your valuable shop time proving to yourself that you can make a proper square stick, grab a board and try it—no one is watching and you just might learn something.

glued to the notched pieces should be cut from the remaining stick with about a 1-inch waste piece between them. As a result, in the assembled puzzle, these two stubs should look like they are really one piece and that the grain pattern is properly aligned and continuous. So, after the two notched pieces have been completed, cut off a 1-inch length from the stick, move the stick a little less than an inch, and cut off another 1-inch length. The two 1-inch pieces are the stubs and the shorter center piece is waste.

Glue the stubs to the notched pieces, being careful to maintain the alignment of the grain. Remember that in the assembled puzzle, the two notched pieces are at 90 degrees to each other. Also, be careful to align the stubs with the edges of the notches. When the glue dries, the two puzzle pieces should fit together with some force—more force than is ultimately desirable, but not enough to dent or damage the wood. To arrive at a perfect fit, tape some 280 grit sandpaper face up onto a flat surface such as a tool table or piece of heavy plate glass (**Figure 8**). Maintaining uniform pressure, rub each side of each puzzle piece on the sandpaper, one or two passes at a time, constantly testing the fit of the two pieces, until you achieve a moderate friction fit.

Now, with the puzzle assembled, using a smooth file, very slightly ease every edge and corner, (except those that are part of the center lap joint) just enough for a good feel. Apply a little oil or wax to enhance the appearance of the wood and provide some protection.

You will know you have achieved success with this project if the two halves do not fall apart on their own, if a typical 10-year-old can apply enough force to take the puzzle apart and put it together, and if there is no visual evidence of the lap joint in the assembled puzzle.

Now, for a real instructive challenge, make this same puzzle again, this time using only hand tools!

Figure 7—A loose and rattling ball bearing in the drilled cavity signals that the burr is meant to be opened.

Figure 8—Size the puzzle pieces by rubbing on 280-grit sandpaper that has been taped to a flat surface such as a machine table.

Figure 9—*The* Pocoloco *puzzle resembles a squared-off wooden ball with pyramidal corner cutouts.*

Figure 10—*The six identical assemblies each consist of three prism-shaped pieces glued together.*

Chapter 2

Pocoloco

Designed by Vinco

Pocoloco, like the *Bi-Burr*, is quite simple in concept and simple to make. But the precision required in cutting the pieces and gluing them together may very well prove to be challenging, and in all likelihood, instructive.

The ball-like finished object, **Figure 9**, is made of six identical assemblies, **Figures 10** and **11,** of three identical pieces—18 elemental pieces in all. These pieces are right angle prisms.

Begin by preparing a square stick 18 inches long and 1 inch on a side (see *Making a Square Stick*, page 18). Then, saw it on a band saw or table saw down a diagonal into two prismatic sticks

(**Figures 12** and **13**). Now make a jig or cradle to hold these long prisms, wide face up, and pass them through a thickness planer (**Figures 14, 15** and **16**). If all the tools used are sharp and well tuned, and if the jig is carefully made, the prisms will be accurately cut and the surfaces free of most visible tool marks.

Hand planing the sides of the square stick and/ or the broad surface of the prismatic sticks may improve the surface finish. Hand planing will remove snipe left by the surface planer, and even improve the dimensional accuracy of the sticks, but it must be done with great care to avoid upsetting the required uniformity. The one thing

Vaclav Obsivac (Vinco)

Vaclav Obsivac (b. 1962) was trained in electronics and worked in the telecommunication industry for 10 years. As a child in school, he was interested in mathematics and geometry and he came from a family of woodworkers. With this combination, it was no surprise that he took an interest in puzzles. Mr. Obsivac is now a full time puzzle designer with a particular interest in Archimedean solids. His puzzles are all constructed from local wood species.

Mr. Obsivac lives in the Czech Republic.

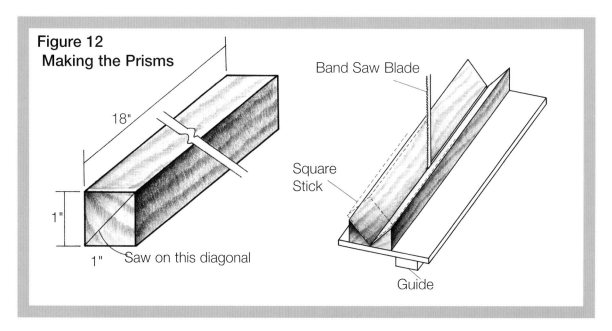

Figure 11—*One piece removed from* Pocoloco.

Figure 12
Making the Prisms

18"

1"

1" Saw on this diagonal

Band Saw Blade

Square
Stick

Guide

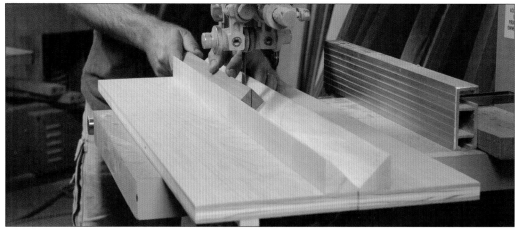

Figure 13—*Saw the square stick down the middle on a diagonal to make two prismatic sticks. This photo shows the band saw set up; a table saw could also be used.*

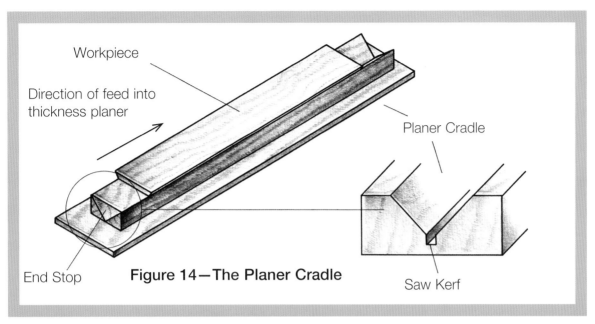

Workpiece

Direction of feed into
thickness planer

Planer Cradle

End Stop

Figure 14—The Planer Cradle

Saw Kerf

Figure 15—The shop-made cradle, with a stop at one end, is being used with a thickness planer.

Figure 16—The long prismatic stick sits in the shop made cradle, ready to be pushed into the thickness planer.

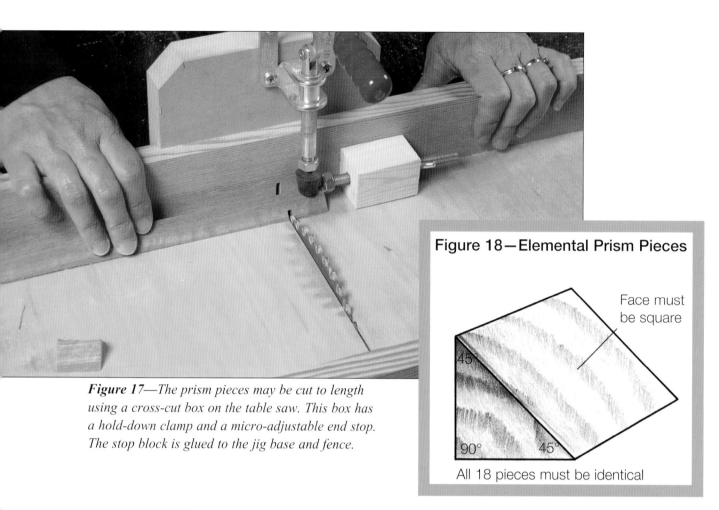

Figure 17—The prism pieces may be cut to length using a cross-cut box on the table saw. This box has a hold-down clamp and a micro-adjustable end stop. The stop block is glued to the jig base and fence.

Figure 18—Elemental Prism Pieces

Face must be square

45°

90°   45°

All 18 pieces must be identical

Figure 19—Make a simple fixture to help glue the puzzle elements together. Finger pressure is enough, until the glue grabs.

you need not worry about at this stage is the absolute size of the sticks, as long as they are both the same. Also, 90 degree angles and 45 degree angles must be spot-on the full length of the sticks, and they must not taper at all.

Now, set up a micro-adjustable stop on your table saw or radial arm saw. A bolt threaded through a slightly undersized hole in a block of wood clamped to the table or fence will work well. (Alternatively, the bolt could pass loosely through a hole in the block, with jam nuts to hold the setting.) The parts must be clamped solidly in place during each cut, perhaps using a stick to hold the part against the fence, in order to prevent catches and kickbacks. This will also keep the parts from being trapped between the saw blade and the stop. Use a back-up board and zero clearance table insert to obtain the cleanest possible cuts. Better yet, build and use a jig like that shown in **Figure 17**. Set the stop at a distance from the saw blade equal to, or as close as you can to, the width of the wide face of the prism. Use a scrap stick for trial cut-offs as you adjust the stop. The objective is to cut off these prism shaped parts so that their large faces are precisely square **(Figure 18)**. This can be checked using a vernier caliper. If you do not have the right measuring tools, hold one cut-off against another, square face to square face but rotated so that they are 90 degrees to one another, and let your fingertips determine if the dimensions of the large faces are the same in both directions.

If necessary, adjust the position of the stop and try again. If you are off, even a little bit, the puzzle will either not go together or else it will fall apart when assembled. When you are satisfied that the length of each prism is right on, cut off the required 18 pieces. At this stage, do not sandpaper any edges or surfaces. Do not tear down your set-ups—you may need them later. The two 18 inch sticks should provide enough material to cover a few mistakes and circumvent the need to endanger your fingers by holding a very short stub near the saw blade.

Glue these 18 pieces into six identical assemblies as shown in **Figure 11**. Use yellow glue, sparingly, applying finger pressure for a minute or so, one joint at a time. Make certain that the edges of all three pieces in each assembly are aligned. This can best be done by preparing a gluing jig with a right angle fence to push against while the glue grabs*, **Figure 19.** In about half an hour, scrape off any squeeze-out. After another hour or so, the glue should be sufficiently set for a trial assembly of the whole puzzle (**Figure 11**). Don't be too surprised if the parts fit too loosely or too tightly. You are looking for a light friction fit of all parts, requiring some force, but not a lot of force, to assemble and disassemble. Attaining that kind of fit is not easy. If your first attempt is unsuccessful, determine what to do differently and try again, using your previous thickness planer and saw cut-off settings as a starting point. It might take several iterations before you are satisfied. Rounding off the edges of the puzzle parts is not required on this project.

* The assembly jig is a simple improvised device, as shown in **Figure 19**. Along one edge of a 3 x 3-inch face of a 1 x 3 x 3-inch block, attach a 1 x 1 x 3-inch fence or stop. Mount the jig in a vise. Push two pieces to be glued against the stop until the glue bites. A little wax or paraffin on the jig will prevent the glue from sticking to it.

Figure 20. Pocoloco, *disassembled. The six parts are identical.*

Figure 21—*It doesn't seem possible, but all four M puzzle pieces will fit inside the box.*

Chapter 3

MMMM

Designed by Hirokazu Iwasawa

Four identical M-shaped pieces must be placed into a box and the lid must then be put on (**Figure 21**). But all the obvious ways of packing the four pieces leave parts of the pieces sticking up too high for the lid to fit. Like all good puzzles, the correct answer is elusive. The puzzle is offered with the four pieces outside the box, or, for a bit more drama, the pieces can be previously fitted correctly in the box which is then turned over in front of your pigeon so that the lid falls off and the pieces dump out without anyone seeing the solution. This presentation assures those watching that the pieces do actually fit. (Although very different in detail, you may note some conceptual similarities between *MMMM* and *Blockhead*.)

If the dimensions shown on the sketches are followed accurately, the puzzle will work just fine. However, small deviations from these dimensions will make the solution a little too easy, a little too hard, or even impossible. So, if you wish to scale the puzzle up or down, do so carefully. Or, if you use material that is thicker or thinner than $\frac{1}{8}$ inch for the M pieces, some adjustments in other dimensions may be required.

The M pieces can be cut from solid wood, plywood, or fiberboard, **Figure 22**. After the rectangular shape is cut, the M can be formed using any of a number of power or handsaws, though with a table saw, some handwork will be required to remove the waste. Clean up any raw

Hirokazu Iwasawa

Hirokazu Iwasawa studied mathematical engineering and philosophy at university. He began to design mechanical puzzles in 2003. Mr. Iwasawa invented a new type of sliding block puzzle that was awarded a prize in the design competition at the 2005 International Puzzle Party. Mr. Iwasawa has been a member of the Academy of Recreational Mathematics,

Japan, since 1986. He lives in Yokohama, Japan.

The *MMMM* puzzle, designed by Mr. Iwasawa, and a puzzle designed by Serhiy Grabarchuk, a Ukrainian puzzle designer, are both based upon the same mathematical idea. Both puzzles were invented independently.

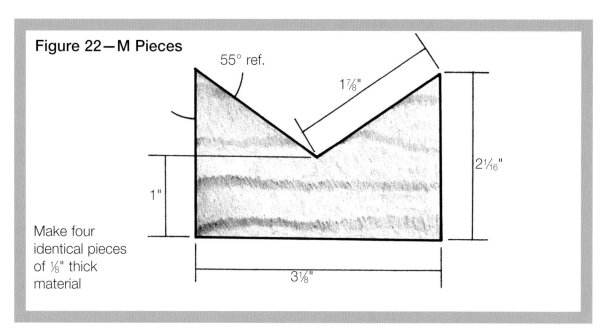

Figure 22—M Pieces

55° ref.

1⁷⁄₈"

2¹⁄₁₆"

1"

3¹⁄₈"

Make four
identical pieces
of ⅛" thick
material

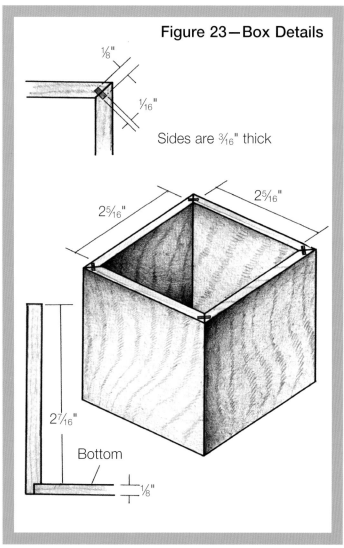

Figure 23—Box Details

⅛"

¹⁄₁₆"

Sides are ³⁄₁₆" thick

2⁵⁄₁₆"

2⁵⁄₁₆"

2⁷⁄₁₆"

Bottom

⅛"

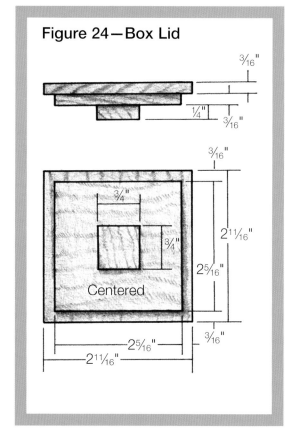

Figure 24—Box Lid

³⁄₁₆"

¼"

³⁄₁₆"

³⁄₁₆"

¾"

¾"

2¹¹⁄₁₆"

Centered

2⁵⁄₁₆"

³⁄₁₆"

2⁵⁄₁₆"

2¹¹⁄₁₆"

edges left by the saw. Very slightly ease the edges of these pieces with sandpaper or a file, being careful not to overdo it since the fit of the pieces in the box could be adversely affected.

The box construction is straightforward (**Figure 23**). Long splines are used with miter joints for the corners, and the bottom is set into rabbets in the lower edges of the sides. The lid, **Figure 24**, has two squares glued to its under side; the larger square ensures alignment of the lid, and the smaller one will foil some possible attempts at false solutions.

The 45-degree miters of the sides can be cut on a table saw (**Figure 25**). Or, you might want to try cutting these miters using a hand plane and miter shooting board (**Figure 26**). Using the thinnest saw blade you can find, possibly $1/16$ inch thick, cut the slots in the bevels for the splines (**Figure 28**). The slots can also be cut on a router table with a $1/16$-inch straight bit. The cross-grain splines are sized to be a sliding fit in the slots. The width of the splines should be just a hair less than twice the depth of the slots. Cut the splines a bit long and clean up the ends after the glue dries. When gluing the corners of the box with the splines in place, heavy rubber bands will work well as clamps, being sure to keep the box square (**Figure 29**). When the glue dries, sand the outside of the box and chamfer or round all corners.

Using thicker or thinner material for the box is perfectly fine, but the inside dimensions of the box should not be altered, unless you are deliberately changing the scale of the puzzle. You may wish to make thicker walls if it is impractical for you to find or prepare thin stock, or if you want to try the long spline miter joints and cannot find a thin

Figure 25—Miter the box sides on the table saw, with the blade set at 45 degrees and with a sacrificial piece of wood clamped to the fence, to minimize torn grain. Watch those fingers!

Figure 26—As an alternative to the table saw method, you can miter the box sides using a hand plane and a miter shooting board, also called a "donkey."

Figure 27—Solve the puzzle by tucking the pieces behind one another.

blade for the splines, necessitating more wall thickness to accommodate a wider slot.

Even when the *MMMM* solution is understood, **Figure 27**, some dexterity will be required to solve the puzzle. If the pieces are just a little loose, you will probably be able to insert one piece at a time into the box, tucking each successive piece under the last. But if a little dimensional carelessness results in the M pieces being somewhat large or the box a bit small, you might have to juggle all four pieces into the proper configuration outside the box and insert them as an assembly. And that can be very tricky!

Figure 28—Cut the spline slot in the face of the 45-degree bevel on the table saw, using the miter guide and the rip fence.

Figure 29—Use heavy rubber bands to clamp the assembled box while the glue dries.

Figure 30—Please Drop In *consists of a flat wooden tray or box with a clear plastic top that is screwed in place, and four trapezoidal pieces. The object is to drop the pieces into the box through the slot. They will fit, left.*

Chapter 4

Please Drop In

Designed by Stewart Coffin

Four trapezoidal puzzle pieces are presented along with, though separate from, a plastic covered frame (**Figure 30**). The objective is to insert each of these pieces into the opening on one side of the frame so that all four pieces fit completely within the frame. Simple. Well, maybe not quite so simple. The solver will probably soon realize that all pieces can fit through the opening in at least one orientation, and may even recognize that the area of the four pieces taken as a whole is about the area within the frame, or possibly a bit smaller; but he or she is then left with the

task of deciding the orientation of each piece and the order of insertion. There are a rather limited number of possibilities, but to the solver, it will seem impossible. There will be an irresistible urge to put the right-angle corners of the pieces into the right-angle corners of the frame. Wrong. Stewart Coffin is far trickier than that. Note, for instance, that what looks like a square frame is in fact slightly rectangular (**Figure 31**).

The four puzzle pieces are simple enough to make, using ½-inch solid stock or high grade

Stewart Coffin

For many years, Stewart Coffin has been inventing and building solid geometrical puzzles. The craftsmanship and originality of their design have won him a devoted following among puzzle enthusiasts and collectors throughout the world. He lives in Massachusetts.

Please Drop In 33

Figure 31—Frame Details

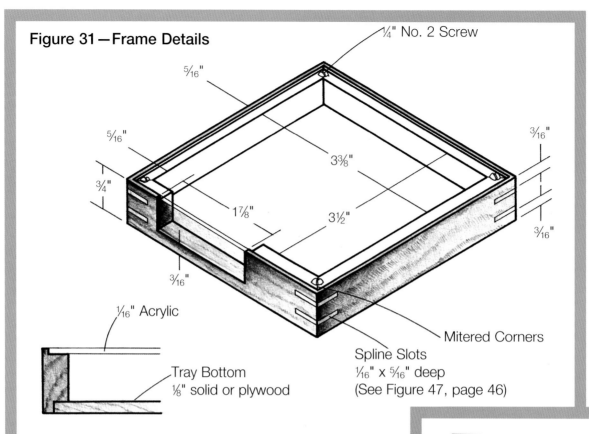

¼" No. 2 Screw

⁵⁄₁₆"

⁵⁄₁₆"

3⅜"

¾"

3½"

1⅞"

³⁄₁₆"

³⁄₁₆"

³⁄₁₆"

³⁄₁₆"

¹⁄₁₆" Acrylic

Tray Bottom
⅛" solid or plywood

Mitered Corners

Spline Slots
¹⁄₁₆" x ⁵⁄₁₆" deep
(See Figure 47, page 46)

Figure 32—Pieces Layout

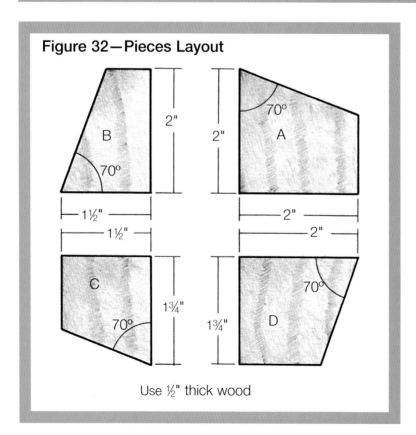

2"

B

70°

1½"

2"

A

70°

2"

1½"

C

70°

1¾"

2"

D

70°

1¾"

Use ½" thick wood

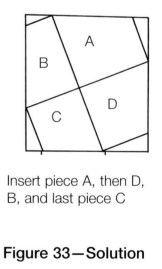

A

B

C

D

Insert piece A, then D,
B, and last piece C

Figure 33—Solution

Figure 34—*The small ledge at the bottom of the opening keeps the pieces inside the frame. However, it also means you have to turn the frame upside-down to remove pieces while you work on the solution.*

plywood (**Figure 32**). But the largest piece must just barely fit through the opening and all must fit totally within the frame, with minimum slop. To accomplish this, one can start by making the frame and then cut the four pieces to just fit, or the pieces can be made first and the frame sized to fit—both approaches will work. Cut the four pieces to the dimensions shown in **Figure 32**, adopting a procedure that enables you to cut all the angled sides with the same set-up. The puzzle pieces should be chamfered on all edges and corners—but go easy, this edge treatment will affect the final fit of the pieces.

Note that the bottom of the opening in the side of the frame is raised just a bit above the frame floor. This step helps ensure that all four pieces are indeed within the frame when the puzzle is correctly solved and that they are less likely to slide out inadvertently (**Figures 33** and **34**).

The corners of the frame in the model made for illustration are mitered with feather splines for looks and strength, but of course, other joints would serve as well. Black walnut was used for the tray parts and the four puzzle pieces were cut from maple. The tray bottom, set into rabbeted edges of the frame, is made of solid wood, but thin plywood would also be satisfactory. The cover is clear acrylic, $\frac{1}{16}$ inch thick, obtainable from plastic supply sources and some hobby shops. Sand the edges of the plastic smooth. This piece of plastic can be simply placed on the top edge of the frame and secured by four small wood screws, or, as in our model, set in rabbets.

Figure 35—Lateral Thinking, *assembled neatly in its tray.*

Figure 36—Lateral Thinking, *with parts dumped out of the tray.*

Chapter 5

Lateral Thinking

Designed by Brian Young

An old paper and pencil puzzle asks you to draw nine dots, three rows of three dots, in a square array, and then connect all nine dots with four straight lines without lifting the pencil from the paper. If you haven't seen it, you might want to try it before reading further—close the book, get a pencil and piece of paper and see if you can solve it.

Are you back? The conventional thought pattern of most people is to see the nine dots as a square and the square is seen as a boundary that none of the connecting lines are allowed to cross, even though extending the lines beyond the square is not prohibited in the statement of the problem. The solution, which requires "going outside the box," can be found in **Figure 40** on page 41.

Another phrase related to "going outside the box" is "lateral thinking," the name Brian Young took for this clever puzzle—you will see why. Actually, the seven pieces (and their tray), **Figures 35** and **36**, that comprise *Lateral*

Brian Young

Brian Young's obsession with puzzles began as a four-year-old, when a favorite uncle gave him his first puzzle. He was instantly hooked, and puzzles became a lifelong addiction.

In the early 1990s, he saw the potential to harness his life's interest to his woodworking skills and establish his profession. So began his full-time enterprise, called Mr. Puzzle, and the years since have been devoted to inventing, making, collecting and playing with puzzles.

Brian is now an internationally recognized puzzle creator whose ingenious handmade works are held in collections around the world. Mr. Young lives in Queensland, Australia.

Figure 37—Dimensions of Puzzle Parts

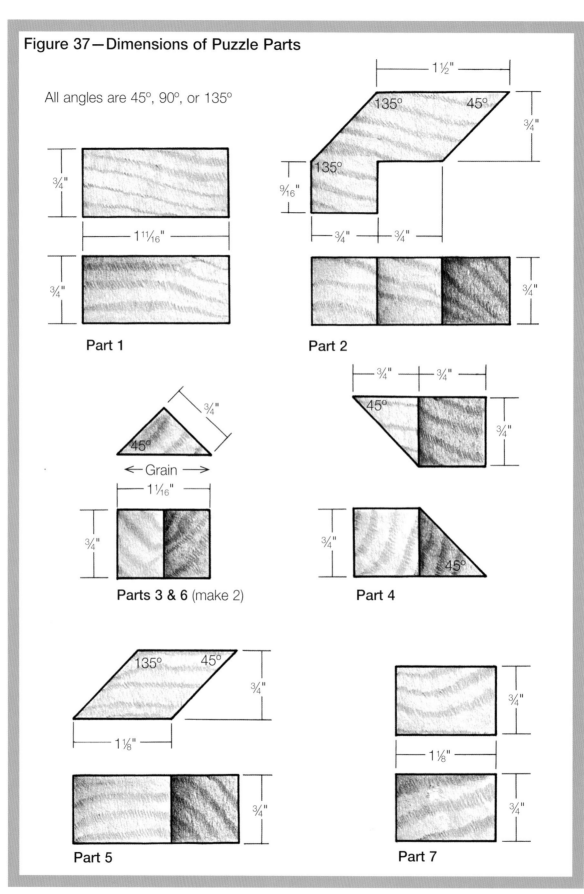

All angles are 45°, 90°, or 135°

Part 1

Part 2

Parts 3 & 6 (make 2)

Part 4

Part 5

Part 7

Thinking can be used for at least four different puzzles:

1. Use all seven pieces to form a letter L. *

2. Use all seven pieces to form a letter T. *

3. Use all seven pieces to form both the letter L and the letter T at the same time. *

4. Put all the pieces back in the tray.

*The dimensions of the vertical and horizontal strokes in all letters are exactly equal and symmetrical.

Lateral thinking is definitely required to solve problem 3!

Six of the seven parts can be cut from a length of ¾ x ¾-inch stock, (see *Making a Square Stick*, on page 18), in a straightforward manner using a table saw, radial-arm saw or chop saw, **Figure 37**. Seriously consider making one or more jigs based on the principles shown in the technical sidebars on pages 60 and 66 to make most of the cut-offs. At a minimum, an adjustable cut-off stop should be used for all square and angled cuts so that all dimensions can be tweaked for accuracy. The two small 45/45/90 prisms, parts Nos. 3, 4, and 6, should be cut with the long side parallel to the grain in order to avoid fragile cross-grain edges. Part No. 2 is only a little trickier for those wanting to make it from one solid piece. It is, of course, possible to make this piece by gluing together two components, each of which can be made from the same ¾ x ¾-inch stick. Caution: When working with these small pieces, please take no chances that might harm your fingers!

The construction of the tray is a bit different from others shown in this book, (although any of a number of designs would work as well). Refer to **Figure 39**. Start with a block of wood 3¼ x 3⁷⁄₁₆ x ¾ inches thick. Select a species that contrasts nicely with the wood chosen for the puzzle pieces. If you are cutting this block from a larger piece,

Figure 38—Use a straight bit in the router table to plow the tray cavity. The two side pieces complete the tray.

you may want to do the routing before parting it from the rest of the material so that you have a larger piece to hold on to while machining the cavity. Using a table-mounted router, cut a ¼-inch deep channel, running in the direction of the grain, as shown in **Figure 38**. To complete the frame, two side pieces must be fashioned and glued into place. Note that one of these pieces has a ¾ x ³⁄₁₆-inch cutout. When the glue sets, the tray can be cleaned up, chamfering or rounding the edges as desired. If you have closely held to the nominal dimensions, the seven puzzle pieces should fit perhaps a little snug in the tray. Lightly sand each part on a flat surface and they should now fit easily, but without much room for movement, then oil the pieces.

The solutions to all four problems are shown in **Figure 40**.

Figure 39—Tray Dimensions

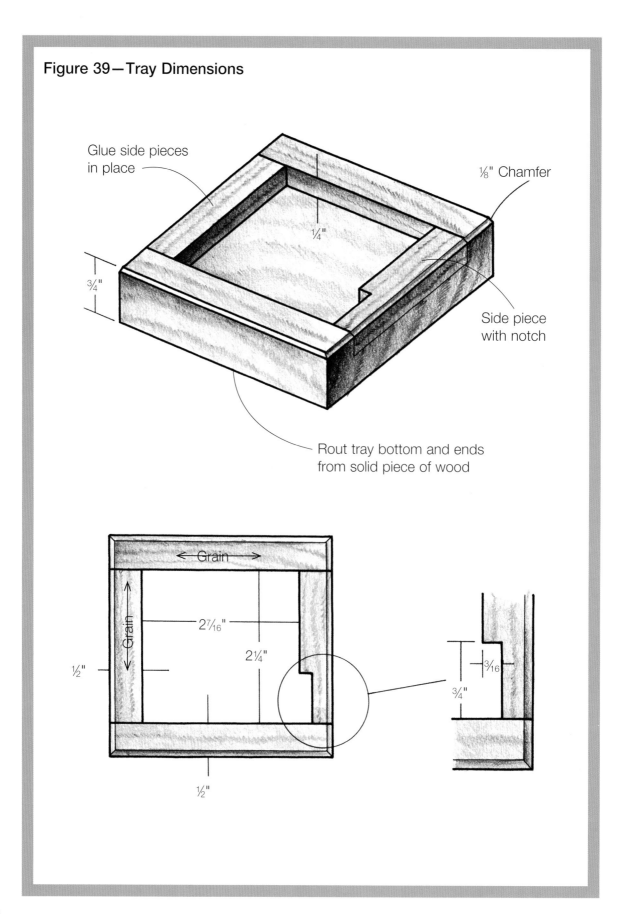

Glue side pieces in place

⅛" Chamfer

¼"

¾"

Side piece with notch

Rout tray bottom and ends from solid piece of wood

← Grain →

Grain

2⁷⁄₁₆"

2¼"

½"

½"

³⁄₁₆"

¾"

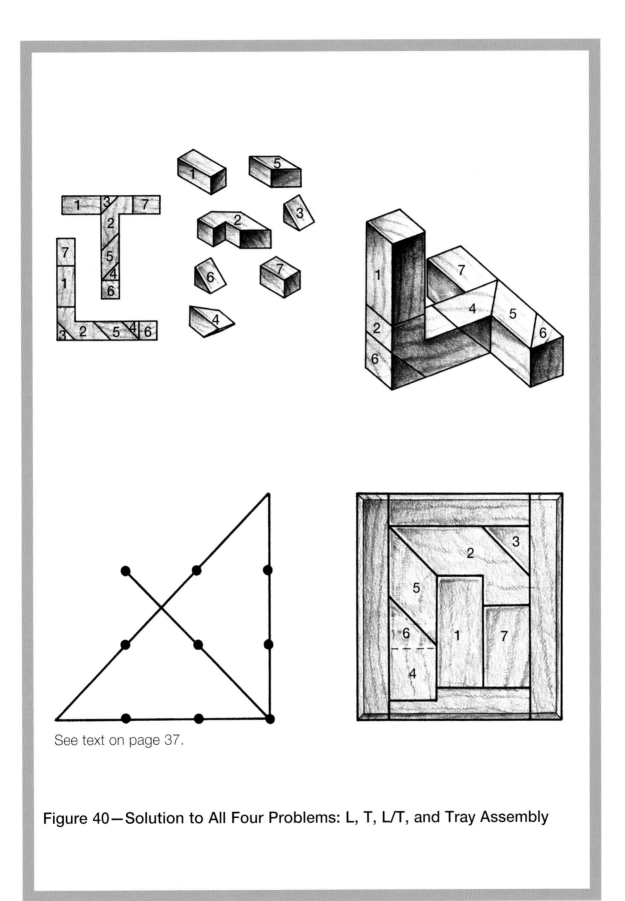

See text on page 37.

Figure 40—Solution to All Four Problems: L, T, L/T, and Tray Assembly

Figure 41—Blockhead. *All four pieces are at home in the box.*

Figure 42—*The four pieces are identical, with sloping sides and 1½"*
square tops.

Chapter 6

Blockhead

Designed by Bill Cutler

Blockhead has nearly every characteristic considered important by serious puzzlers for a good puzzle design. There are a small number of pieces, it is simple in concept, the objective is immediately evident, all the obvious ways of solving the puzzle do not work, and the real solution is elusive and surprising. The judges at the 1986 Hikimi puzzle competition recognized the merits of his design (**Figure 41**) by awarding Bill the grand prize.

Fortunately, making *Blockhead* is not as difficult as is solving it. Four identical blocks must be packed into an open box such that the tops are all flat and level with the edges of the box. These blocks are cube-like, but not true cubes—some of the corners are right angles, and some are not. One face on each block is a true square, and the rest are not.

Begin by preparing a stick about 12 inches long, having the trapezoidal cross sectional shape and dimensions shown in **Figure 43**. Hold to the dimensions closely. For the model shown in **Figure 41**, Indian rosewood was used for the blocks and oak for the box, but virtually any

Bill Cutler

Bill Cutler has had a life-long interest in mechanical puzzles, particularly interlocking burr puzzles and box-packing puzzles. He has a PhD in mathematics from Cornell University, and has been employed for the last 27 years as a computer programmer. He has combined these interests by writing computer programs to analyze box-packing and interlocking puzzles and is particularly interested in using such programs to design new puzzles.

Mr. Cutler lives in Illinois.

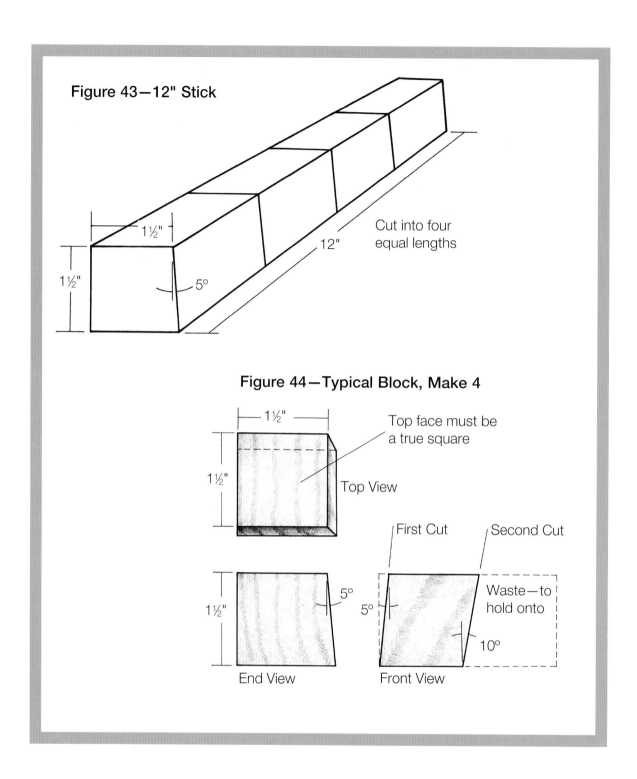

Figure 43—12" Stick

1½"

1½"

12"

5°

Cut into four
equal lengths

Figure 44—Typical Block, Make 4

1½"

1½"

Top face must be
a true square

Top View

First Cut

Second Cut

1½"

5°

End View

5°

Front View

Waste—to
hold onto

10°

species will work—even softer wood is okay since the puzzle is so robust. Cut the stick into four equal lengths. The reason for doing this will become clear in a moment. Each piece, approximately 3 inches long, will become one of the four puzzle pieces.

Next, set up your radial arm saw to take a cut at a 5-degree angle as shown in **Figure 45**. (**Figure 45** is shown without the blade guard for clarity. Be certain your safety attachments are all in use, if at all possible, and take extreme caution if operating your power tools with these attachments temporarily removed.) The workpiece should be held against the fence oriented as shown in **Figure 45**. Cut the left end of each of the four workpieces at this 5-degree angle. Re-set the blade angle to 10-degrees. Set up the stop and adjust it so that the second cut leaves the top of each block exactly square (**Figure 44**). Cut all four blocks. We started with workpieces that were much longer than were dimensionally required in order to have stock to hold onto for these cuts. Using a table saw for these cut-offs, rather than a radial-arm saw, would require a slightly different set up, but the method is similar.

The blocks are now essentially finished, except perhaps for some light sanding on a flat surface to clean up saw marks. A very light chamfer on all edges will make the blocks more pleasant to handle.

The box that these four pieces must fit into is much like other boxes or trays used with other puzzles, but with an important difference. The inside surfaces of the sides are all beveled inward, or undercut, at 5 degrees (**Figures 48** and **49**) Without this undercut, one could insert all four pieces, but it would be impossible to maneuver the tops of all the blocks into the same flat plane, flush with the top edge of the box. Prepare a piece of stock ¾ x 1⅝ x at least 20 inches long. Rabbet one edge as shown in **Figure 48** to receive the

Figure 45—*The shop-made hold-down locks the short stick against the fence of the radial-arm saw. With this set-up, the saw blade is tilted to 5° for the first cut on each piece. Then, the stop is moved, the saw is reset to a 10° tilt, and the second cut is made. When the stop is perfectly positioned for the second cut, the top of each block will be exactly square.*

Figure 46—*This jig cuts the spline slots in the box body. It's guided by the table saw's rip fence.*

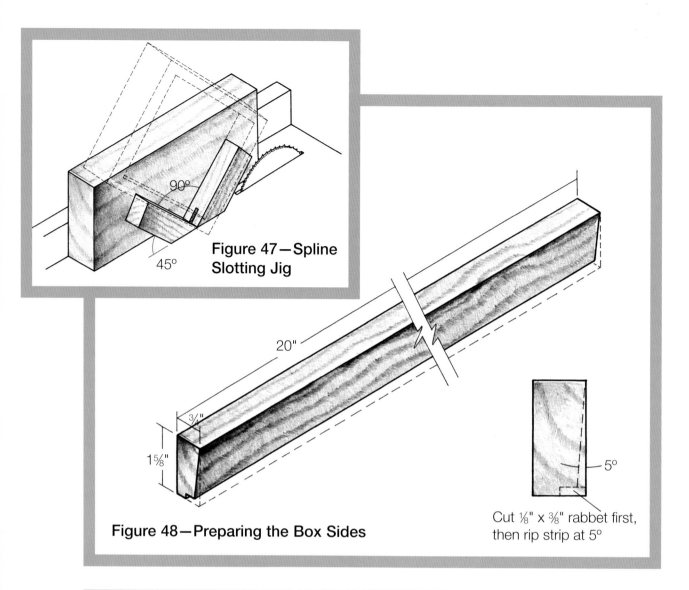

90°

45°

Figure 47—Spline
Slotting Jig

20"

¾"

1⅝"

Figure 48—Preparing the Box Sides

5°

Cut ⅛" x ⅜" rabbet first,
then rip strip at 5°

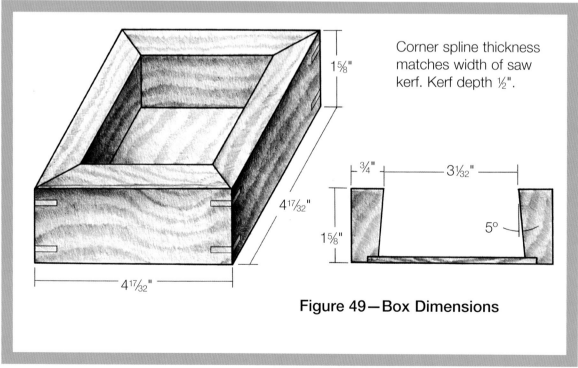

Corner spline thickness
matches width of saw
kerf. Kerf depth ½".

1⅝"

4¹⁷⁄₃₂"

4¹⁷⁄₃₂"

¾"

3¹⁄₃₂"

1⅝"

5°

Figure 49—Box Dimensions

bottom of the box. Rip the 5-degree bevel on a table saw. Cut the pieces to length and then miter the ends, or simply cut the miters directly. It is important that the opening at the top of the box be about $\frac{1}{32}$ inch larger in both directions than twice the dimension of one side of the square face of the blocks. Glue the four sides together—a strap clamp, rubber bands, or tape will provide sufficient pressure until the glue dries. The bottom can be made of solid wood or plywood $\frac{1}{8}$ inch thick, cut to fit the rabbeted opening, and glued in place. To strengthen the corners of the box and add a bit of decoration, you could add feather splines. A simple jig will facilitate cutting the slots for the splines, **Figures 46** and **47**. Lightly ease all edges of the completed box.

To solve the puzzle, place all four blocks on a table with their square sides on top. Arrange them loosely in a two-by-two square. Rotate each piece so that the faces that slant 5 degree off vertical are all on the outside of the assembly, **Figure 50**. Now, pick up all four blocks at the same time by holding them with both hands at their bottoms— they will scrunch in—and drop them, all at once, into the box (**Figure 51**). The blocks should all settle in and leave a flat surface at the top of the box, as shown in **Figure 41**.

Figure 50—*To solve the puzzle, arrange the four puzzle pieces on table surface, in a square array, with their square sides on top and their outer faces all sloping outward.*

Figure 51—*Lift all four blocks at once, then drop them, all at once, into the box.*

Figure 52—The completed Aha Box, *closed. This box is made of oak with a walnut inlay.*

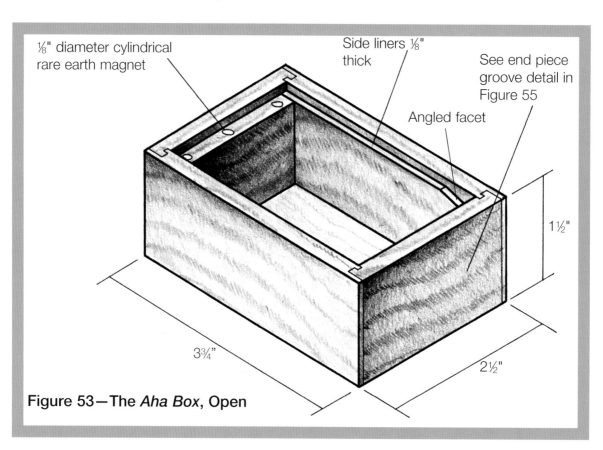

⅛" diameter cylindrical rare earth magnet

Side liners ⅛" thick

See end piece groove detail in Figure 55

Angled facet

1½"

3¾"

2½"

Figure 53—The *Aha Box*, Open

Chapter 7

Aha Box

Designed by Allan Boardman

Other boxes in this collection of puzzles are intended to establish a specific volume in which to pack the puzzle pieces or simply provide a nice looking container to hold them. The *Aha Box*, **Figure 52**, is just a box, but one that employs a gimmick to get it opened—a trick box. Finding that gimmick is the task presented to the solver. This box is intended to be displayed, perhaps on a coffee table, inviting a guest to pick it up and attempt to open it. You might deliberately place something inside—a relic, some coins, a

favorite beach pebble—that would rattle around, increasing the curiosity of your guest. The solution to opening the box is simple enough, but far from obvious. Of course, boxes of all sorts, whether they require trick opening methods or not, are favorite projects of many woodworkers, and the construction methods used for this puzzle are readily applicable to countless other designs.

The solution requires finding just the right place on the lid to press. Applying sufficient pressure to

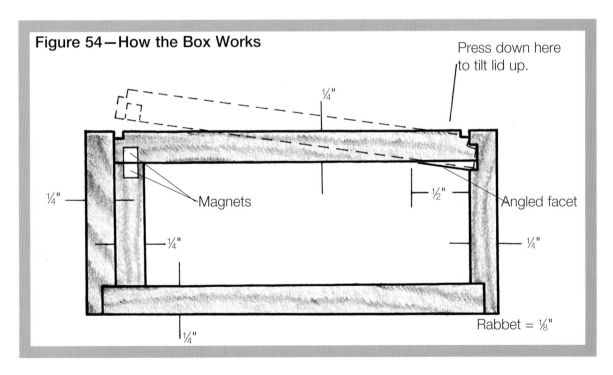

Figure 54—How the Box Works

Press down here to tilt lid up.

¼"

Magnets

¼"

¼"

½"

Angled facet

¼"

¼"

Rabbet = ⅛"

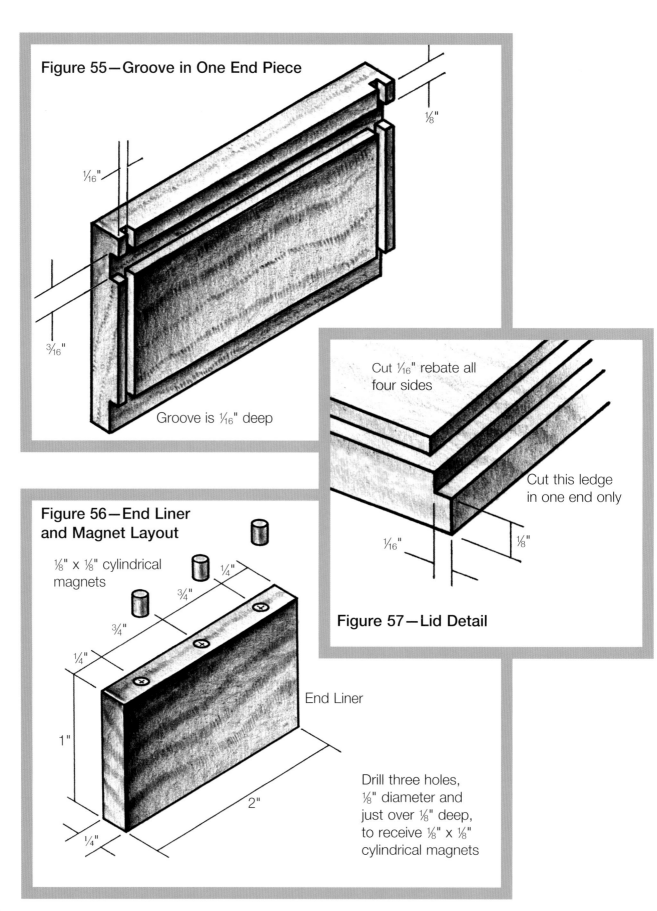

Figure 55—Groove in One End Piece

1/8"

1/16"

3/16"

Groove is 1/16" deep

Cut 1/16" rebate all four sides

Cut this ledge in one end only

1/16"

1/8"

Figure 57—Lid Detail

Figure 56—End Liner and Magnet Layout

1/8" x 1/8" cylindrical magnets

1/4"

3/4"

3/4"

1/4"

1"

2"

1/4"

End Liner

Drill three holes, 1/8" diameter and just over 1/8" deep, to receive 1/8" x 1/8" cylindrical magnets break apart hidden small, but powerful, magnets will cause the lid to tilt up and be easy to remove. Before getting started on the construction, locate a source on the Internet that deals in rare earth magnets. You will need six ⅛ x ⅛-inch cylindrical magnets.

Rabbet and dado joints were used for the corners of the box, **Figure 60**, but this might be a good project for you to try mini-finger joints, using a ⅛-inch straight bit with your router table, or any of the other box corner joints shown throughout this book. The stock required for most of this project is ¼ inch thick. If you do not have the tools necessary to prepare this stock—a band saw for re-sawing and a thickness planer for cleaning up the saw marks and achieving the desired thickness—there are woodworker sources that can supply thin material. However, be aware that purchased thin boards often come cupped and/or distorted and can be difficult to use. When you prepare your own material, on the other hand, you can use thicker stock that has been lying around for a while, stabilized in your shop's environment before it is flattened, re-sawn, and planed to thickness. This doesn't guarantee that you will end up with flat and stable thin stock, but it increases the likelihood. For this project, you will need about one-half a square foot of ¼-inch stock, and about 20 square inches of ⅛-inch stock, assuming, of course, that you use the overall box dimensions given. Having a little extra on hand would provide good insurance.

After laying out the parts to feature the nicest grain patterns on the top and sides, cut the four sides to size, using a zero clearance insert in your table saw to minimize tear-out. Use a ¹⁄₁₆-inch straight bit with your table mounted router, **Figure 59**, to cut the dado in the end pieces, and a ⅛-inch bit to cut the joint details in the side pieces as shown in **Figure 61**. Now cut the rabbet in the edges of the four sides to receive the box bottom. A shallow groove will be required near the inside top edge of one of the end pieces—this can be made with the same router table set-up, adjusting the depth of cut and fence position as

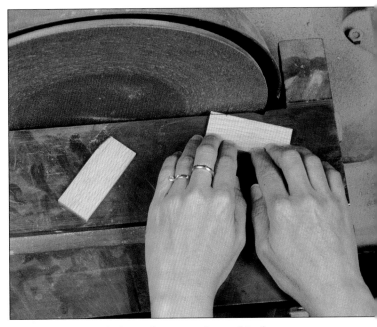

Figure 58—The disk sander, or a sharp chisel, will cut the small angle on the side liner pieces.

needed (**Figure 55**). Lightly sand the inside faces of the four sides and glue them together, making sure that the corners remain square and aligned. Scrape off any glue that has squeezed out, both inside the box as well as in the corners of the bottom rabbets. Cut the bottom to form a snug fit and sand the inside surface. A bench hook and well-tuned hand plane provide a controlled way of approaching that perfect fit (see *Bench Hook*, page 54). Glue the bottom in place.

Two side liners are cut from ⅛-inch stock. The small angled facets shown in **Figure 54** allow the lid to be tilted for opening—they can be made by marking out the slanted line and touching the pieces to a disk sander (**Figure 58**). They should both be identical. The exposed surfaces of these two pieces can now be sanded and the pieces glued in place. Use glue sparingly and hold the parts in position with small spring clamps. Prepare a piece of ¼-inch material, as shown in **Figure 56**, to be glued into one end of the box, the end opposite the grooved end. Drill three ⅛-inch holes a hair more than ⅛ inch deep into the top edge of this piece to receive the magnets.

Figure 59—Use the table mounted router with a 1/16-inch bit to cut the dado for the corner joints of the box.

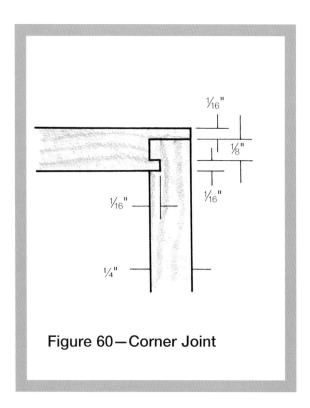

Figure 60—Corner Joint

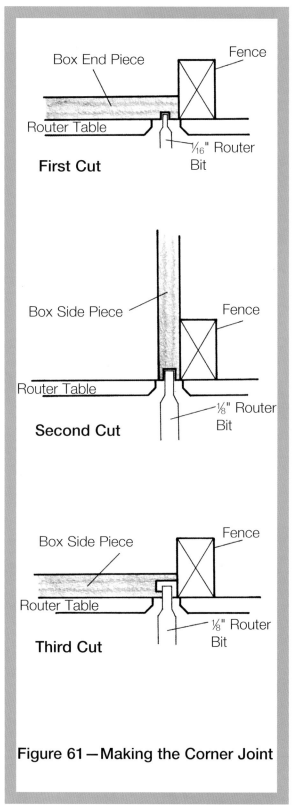

First Cut

Box End Piece

Fence

Router Table

1/16" Router Bit

Second Cut

Box Side Piece

Fence

Router Table

1/8" Router Bit

Third Cut

Box Side Piece

Fence

Router Table

1/8" Router Bit

Figure 61—Making the Corner Joint

Make sure that the magnetic poles of the three magnets are oriented the same way and insert them in the holes so that they are flush with the top of the piece. A tiny drop of glue will ensure that they stay in place. Glue this internal end piece into position as shown in **Figure 54**. The two internal side pieces and this end piece should form a continuous ledge around three sides of the box on which the lid will sit.

To make the lid, cut a piece of the ¼-inch stock so that it is an exact fit to the inside width of the box and ¹⁄₁₆ inch too long to fit lengthwise. Rout the rabbet or ledge on one end of the lid. Again, using your router table set-up with a ⅛-inch bit cut the tiny decorative rabbets, as shown in **Figure 57**. Three ⅛-inch holes, just over ⅛ inch deep should now be drilled into the underside of the lid, taking care that they are exactly opposite the three magnets that have already been installed in the box end piece. Glue the magnets into the holes, again checking that the polarity is correct so that all the magnet pairs attract each other.

At this point, you might wish to decorate the box with a simple inlay as shown in **Figure 52**. To do this, set up your router table with a ¹⁄₁₆-inch bit to cut a groove about ¹⁄₁₆-inch deep. Adjust the fence to cut the long grooves, using an adjustable stop to limit the cut at both ends. Note that the ¹⁄₁₆-inch ledge at one end of the lid means that you will have to do some repositining of the stop and the fence as you rout the four grooves, in order to symmetrically center the inlay. Square up the corners of the grooves with a sharp chisel (**Figure 62**).

Prepare a ¹⁄₁₆ x ¹⁄₁₆-inch strip of contrasting wood to inlay in the grooves—a snug fit is desirable. Cut four pieces of the strip to length and miter the corners with a chisel or razor blade. Apply a bit of glue in the grooves and insert the pieces, tapping them into place with a scrap block and light hammer. Leave them just a bit proud, to be sanded flush after the glue dries.

When the lid is put into place, there should be no

Figure 62—Rout the groove for the inlay in the box lid, and clean up the corners with a small sharp chisel.

crack or space showing around its edges. In fact, there should be no visible clue about how the lid is to be removed. If the fit of the lid is just a bit too snug, try planing a very thin shaving off a binding edge, using the bench hook. When all is just right, the lid will snap shut and will stay in place with no play. Sand all exterior surfaces and the inside of the lid smooth, and round or chamfer the edges of the box to taste.

To open the box, press at one end, or the other, of the lid to tilt it up.

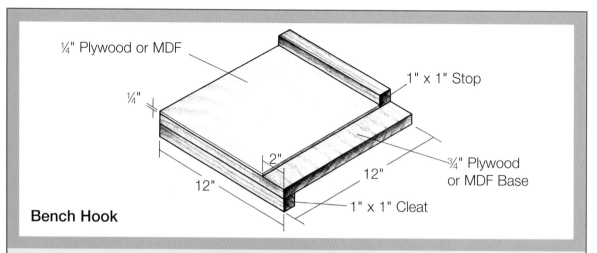

¼" Plywood or MDF

¼"

1" x 1" Stop

2"

12"

¾" Plywood or MDF Base

12"

1" x 1" Cleat

Bench Hook

Bench Hook

Some classical hand tool woodworking methods should be a part of the repertoire of every woodworker, even those totally enchanted with power tools. Why? Because certain operations are better done by tools and procedures in use for hundreds of years before the invention of electricity than by methods employing power tools. Yes, better—and often faster, safer, and quieter as well. Trimming an edge of a small piece of wood to obtain a perfect fit using a bench hook and bench plane is one example.

The bench hook shown here is a simple shop aid that can be used to hold parts in place without a clamp while sawing or planing them. Many types of this kind of fixture have been used in past centuries—for shooting the edge of a board, cutting and trimming a miter, or trimming a piece to fit. It is just about impossible to find these bench aids for sale, so one must make them—a simple enough project.

In use with a plane, the workpiece is held against the stop, slightly overhanging the edge of the platform, and the plane, laid on its side, takes off a shaving. This arrangement removes one degree of freedom from the planing operation, ensuring that the edge is square to the surface of the piece—assuming that the plane is set to take a uniform cut and its sides are square with its sole. If the plane is well tuned and the cutting iron is sharp (these are whole other topics!), the part can be reduced 0.001 inch or so with each pass. This reliably permits the worker to approach and attain a perfect fit—very desirable when making small household items and especially so when making mechanical puzzles. Slight tapers can be added or removed from the workpiece by starting or ending the cut part way through the plane stroke, in case the part being worked is just a bit wide at one end only. Try it, you'll like it!

The bench hook is invaluable when dimensioning a small project part.

Chapter 8

Nob's Neverending Puzzle

Designed by Nob Yoshigahara

Although originally conceived as a packing puzzle, that is, a puzzle that challenges the solver to put all the parts into a container, Nob realized that the parts of his design could be put together in many interesting ways, not just the cube that he had first imagined. Expert puzzle solvers now agree that there are only eleven good shapes that can be made with the parts, but at first, Nob didn't recognize any limit, so he named his creation "neverending" (**Figure 63**, next page).

The elemental building block of this puzzle is half of a cube, the cube being cut on a compound bias (**Figure 65**). Sixteen identical pieces are cut and glued together to form eight similar but different puzzle parts. All of the pieces can be cut from a single 1-inch square stick about 24 inches long, or from two shorter sticks. Scrape or plane the stick smooth, but keep the edges crisp. The 1¼-inch dimension is not essential, but it is critical that the cross-section be exactly square and uniform for its full length (see *Making a Square Stick*, page 18).

The method demonstrated in the photos and figures makes use of a radial arm saw and a special jig (see *Cut-Off Jig*, page 60) for cutting off the puzzle pieces from the stick, but a chop saw or table saw will do the job as well, though

with some modification to the jig design. To cut the angled end of the stick, it is held in a V-shaped cradle glued to the base of the jig at an 82-degree angle to the saw blade. This angle, 82 degrees, results from the dimensions shown in **Figure 65**. This angle can be off a bit and not affect the way the puzzle works. With this arrangement, the angled end and the square end of each piece can be cut alternately without disturbing the set-up. Glued to the cradle, a micro-adjustable end stop makes it easy to get the length of each piece just right. A hold-down arm prevents each block from being kicked back as it is cut free, and enables you to keep your fingers safely away from the saw blade. Set the depth of the saw blade to just barely cut into the base of the jig.

If your saw is aligned and you are using a sharp, quality blade, the pieces should require little clean up. But, if you are left with slight saw marks, tape a sheet of fine sandpaper on a flat surface and rub with light and even pressure to sand them off.

With the jig clamped in place, make a square cut holding the work piece against the fence. Adjust the cut-off stop by eye for a test of the angled cut. When set correctly, two pieces will stack together to

Figure 63—Nob's Neverending Puzzle *consists of eight L-shaped pieces.*

Figure 64—This simple fixture helps glue the puzzle elements together, by allowing you to push the pieces against the table and a stop.

form a perfect cube. If sandpapering the end grain to remove saw marks is required, be sure you factor in the sanding when you test the trial pieces for length. In principle, you could add another micro-adjustable stop to the jig or saw fence to make the square cut, but it is easier to simply cut the angled end of the stick square, wasting as little as possible, before placing it back into the jig's V-cradle for the next angled cut. That way, there is only one stop to adjust and all pieces will be identical. When you are sure that you have an exact setting for the end-stop, cut all sixteen pieces. If you wish to round or chamfer the edges of each piece, just a tiny bit to make them feel nicer, you should wait until the pieces have been glued so that you ease only the exposed edges.

Glue the sixteen pieces in pairs as shown in **Figure 66**, making eight different assemblies. Use very little glue to avoid excess squeeze-out. Finger pressure for a few moments is enough in the way of clamping, but it is best to prepare a flat gluing surface with a stop to have something to press against and align the pieces until the glue grabs, **Figure 64**.

A lidded, or un-lidded, box with $2^{19}/_{32}$ x $2^{19}/_{32}$ x $2^{19}/_{32}$-inch inside dimensions makes a nice storage container for the puzzle parts, and requires that you solve the cube puzzle. Alternately, the puzzle

parts can be stored in a shallow $3^{25}/_{32}$ x $3^{25}/_{32}$-inch tray, which fits the square-donut and the square-with-the-corner-missing puzzle configurations. Both the box and the tray can be made using the suggestions given for other puzzles in this book. Perhaps now is the time for you to create your own box or tray design! Of course, you can also keep the eight puzzle parts in an old sock, but where's the woodworking fun in that?

All eleven solutions found by Nob and his colleague Kozy Kitajima using these parts can be seen in **Figure 68**. Perhaps you can find more interesting shapes that the experts have missed.

Figure 65—Elemental Half-Cube

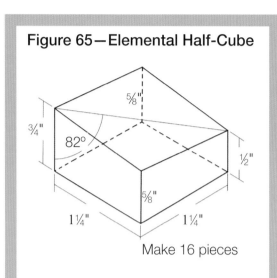

Make 16 pieces

These dimensions may vary, but it is critical that when two of these elemental half-cubes are stacked together, they form an exact cube.

Figure 66—Eight Puzzle Pieces

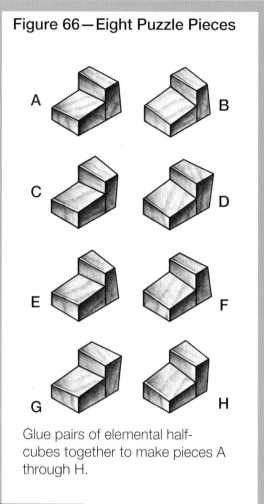

Glue pairs of elemental half-cubes together to make pieces A through H.

Figure 67—The eight puzzle pieces pack neatly into their box, but this is not the only solution.

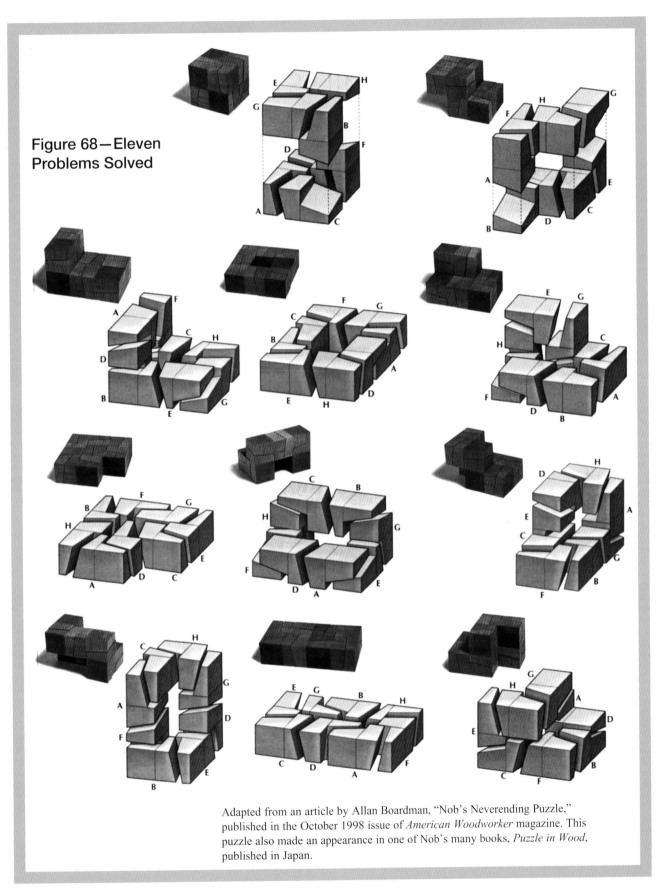

Figure 68—Eleven Problems Solved

Adapted from an article by Allan Boardman, "Nob's Neverending Puzzle," published in the October 1998 issue of *American Woodworker* magazine. This puzzle also made an appearance in one of Nob's many books, *Puzzle in Wood*, published in Japan.

This versatile cut-off jig can work with the radial-arm saw or the chop saw. As shown it is built to cut off the parts for Nob's Neverending Puzzle, *but with modifications it can be used to safely cut off any small duplicate parts.*

Cut-Off Jig

It's often the case that more time can be spent designing and building the required jig or jigs than is actually spent cutting the parts. But in this case, at least, it is well worth the effort. The jig shown, or one like it, will ensure uniform and identical parts. The sloping sides of the V-cradle reduce the saw blade tear-out to a minimum by backing up each cut. The adjustable stop makes fine tuning the length of the parts very simple. The hold-down keeps your fingers safe and prevents the parts from flying off the saw table and bouncing around the shop. And the dual station set-up enables you to make all cuts required by *Nob's Neverending Puzzle*, both square and angled, with no adjustments between cuts. The wedge-shaped plywood spacer base can be made at various angles to suit different projects.

All safety measures and equipment must be utilized whenever possible. If the blade guard on your machine must be removed for a specific operation such as the one shown, be certain that your jig is solidly mounted, all scraps and debris are cleared away, the workpiece is secured, and fingers and hands are a safe distance from the blade.

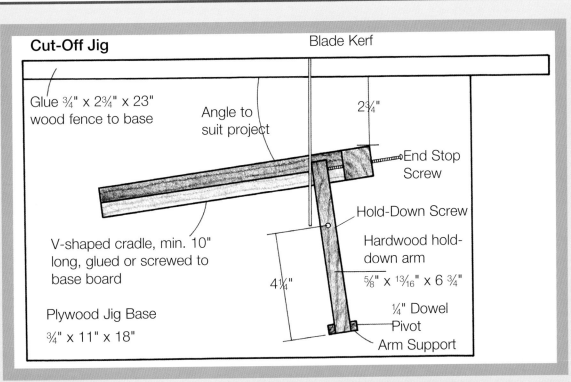

Cut-Off Jig

Blade Kerf

Glue ¾" x 2¾" x 23" wood fence to base

Angle to suit project

2¾"

End Stop Screw

Hold-Down Screw

Hardwood hold-down arm
⅝" x ¹³⁄₁₆" x 6 ¾"

V-shaped cradle, min. 10" long, glued or screwed to base board

4¼"

Plywood Jig Base
¾" x 11" x 18"

¼" Dowel Pivot

Arm Support

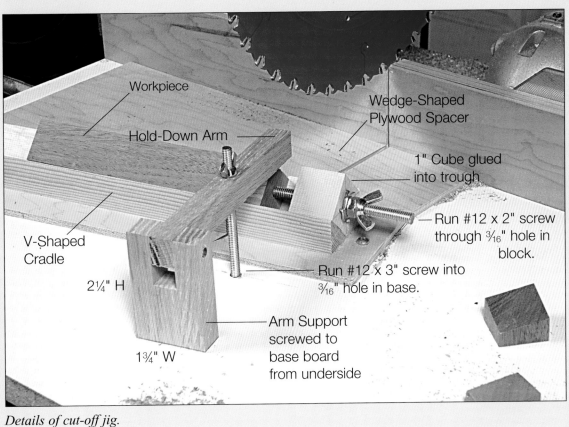

Workpiece

Hold-Down Arm

Wedge-Shaped Plywood Spacer

1" Cube glued into trough

V-Shaped Cradle

2¼" H

Run #12 x 2" screw through ³⁄₁₆" hole in block.

Run #12 x 3" screw into ³⁄₁₆" hole in base.

Arm Support screwed to base board from underside

1¾" W

Details of cut-off jig.

Figure 69—Fifth Avenue *fits neatly in its tray, with all five wood colors in each row and column.*

Figure 70—*Fifth Avenue* Solution

1	4	2	3	5
5	2	3	1	4
4	1	5	2	3
3	5	1	4	2
2	3	4	5	1

Chapter 9

Fifth Avenue

Designed by Nob Yoshigahara

Twenty-five cubes are glued together to make nine puzzle parts—seven parts use three cubes and two use two cubes. But the twenty-five cubes are made from five different species of wood. Although any five species will work, the finished puzzle is all the more enjoyable to play with if all species are easily distinguished from the others by their colors and/or grain patterns. The object of the puzzle is to arrange these nine parts in a five-by-five array such that each row and each column has one cube of each of the five species. There are many ways to make a five-by-five array with these nine parts, but only one way, ignoring mirror images and rotations, of correctly solving the puzzle (**Figure 69**).

Prepare five sticks, each about 8 inches long, one of each kind, or color, of wood. Their cross section should be an exact square, measuring ¾ inch on a side, **Figure 71** (see *Making a Square Stick*, page 18). You can vary this basic dimension considerably, but all sticks must be the same. The sides of the sticks should be planed or scraped smooth to remove any noticeable saw marks while being careful to maintain squareness and uniformity. Of course, this clean-up can be done after cutting the cubes, but that would require more work.

Set up a stop on your table saw or radial arm saw to cut off the cubes. Use the width of one of the sticks as a gage so that the cut-off length is exactly the same as the width of the stick, ensuring that you end up with accurate cubes. The stop must be set up so that the cut-off piece, the cube, is not trapped between the saw blade and the stop or fence, as this could cause the cube to jam or be kicked back—a potentially dangerous safety hazard (**Figures 74** and **75**). Use a zero clearance insert in the saw table and a back-up board to minimize tear-out. Or, to solve all these potential problems—safety hazard, tear-out, dimensional errors—take the time to make a version of the cut-off jig shown on page 66.

You should now have five cubes of five different, contrasting species, twenty-five cubes in all. The end grain of each cube may need a bit of clean-up to remove saw marks, but note that some of these ends will be glued. To avoid the unnecessary sanding of these hidden surfaces (less work and less chance of altering the dimensions), do not sand the end grain until the parts have been glued together.

Although not strictly necessary, the edges of the cubes might be chamfered both for feel and looks. This detail will also hide slight dimensional inaccuracies from cube to cube. If you choose to do this, it should be accomplished before gluing

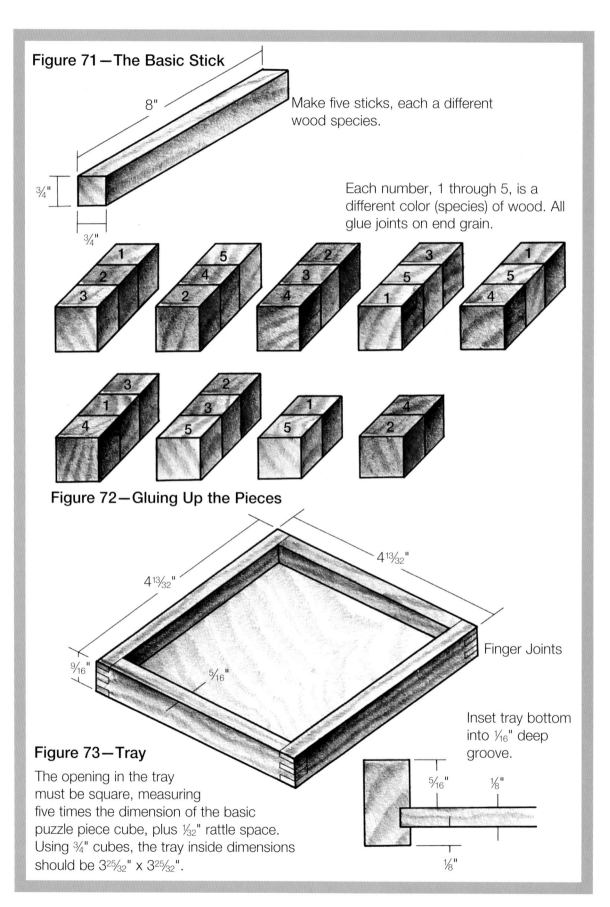

Figure 71—The Basic Stick

8"

3/4"

3/4"

Make five sticks, each a different wood species.

Each number, 1 through 5, is a different color (species) of wood. All glue joints on end grain.

Figure 72—Gluing Up the Pieces

4¹³⁄₃₂"

4¹³⁄₃₂"

9⁄₁₆"

5⁄₁₆"

Finger Joints

Inset tray bottom into ¹⁄₁₆" deep groove.

5⁄₁₆"

⅛"

⅛"

Figure 73—Tray

The opening in the tray must be square, measuring five times the dimension of the basic puzzle piece cube, plus ¹⁄₃₂" rattle space. Using ¾" cubes, the tray inside dimensions should be 3²⁵⁄₃₂" x 3²⁵⁄₃₂".

the cubes together. This can be a tricky operation since the parts are so small. Depending on the method you use to make these chamfers, they can be cut on the edges of the sticks before the sticks are cut into cubes, leaving only the end chamfers for later. The chamfers should all be the same and uniform; free-hand filing or sanding is not likely to produce a quality look. One method that might be used involves a chamfer plane, a very useful tool sold by most Japanese tool dealers. A disk sander can be used to make the chamfers, but some sort of fixture must be devised and used for safety and to obtain uniform results (**Figure 76**).

Glue the cubes together as shown in **Figure 72**, end grain to end grain. Now lightly sand the exposed end grain to remove any visible saw marks. After applying a penetrating oil to increase the contrast between the five wood types, the puzzle is really complete. However, a tray to hold these nine pieces will enhance the presentation, make solving the puzzle more pleasing, and will keep all the parts together when not in use.

The sides of the tray (**Figure 73**) are cut from a stick measuring ⁵⁄₁₆-inch by ⁷⁄₁₆-inch in cross section. Any corner joint can be used—miter, butt, lap, splined, etc. The inside of the tray should allow about ¹⁄₃₂ inch of slop so that the puzzle pieces can easily be inserted and removed. The bottom of the tray can be simply glued to the bottom of the sides or set into a rabbet or groove, depending on the preference of the maker. In the model prepared for this book, the corners of the tray were finger jointed and the bottom, a sheet of ¹⁄₈-inch plywood, was set into a groove.

The solution of *Fifth Avenue* is shown in **Figure 70**.

This puzzle has appeared in one of Nob's many books, *Puzzle in Wood* (sic), published in Japan. Although it might be somewhat less elegant as a woodworking project, instead of using five different species, a single kind of wood can be used, applying stains or dyes to create the different colors needed. *Fifth Avenue* will still be an elegant puzzle.

Figure 74—On the table saw, cut the cubes to length using an offset stop attached to the table surface with cyanoacrylate glue

Figure 75—Cut the cubes to length using a fence stop and improvised holding clamp.

Figure 76—This fixture was designed to hold cubes and limit the depth of cut when making chamfers on the disk sander.

Cut-Off and Notching Jig

Jigs of this general form are a great convenience when making small parts that have to be accurately notched or cut off—two common operations encountered in puzzle making. Although some general guidelines are shown in the drawings, the actual dimensions of the jig must be tailored to your table saw. The features of this jig include zero clearance for the saw blade and a back-up bar (the fence) behind the cut—both will minimize tear-out and swarf. The end stop can be adjusted accurately by trial and error over the needed range of movement for the project at hand, and the workpiece can be safely held in place while making the cut.

Make the sled of any available lumber, being careful that the two bars or fences are straight and have square edges. The bottom can be made of plywood or MDF, ¼ inch thick. The slide bars should be hardwood, carefully trimmed for a no-play sliding fit in the miter slots. Glue the slide bars to the underside of the sled square to the

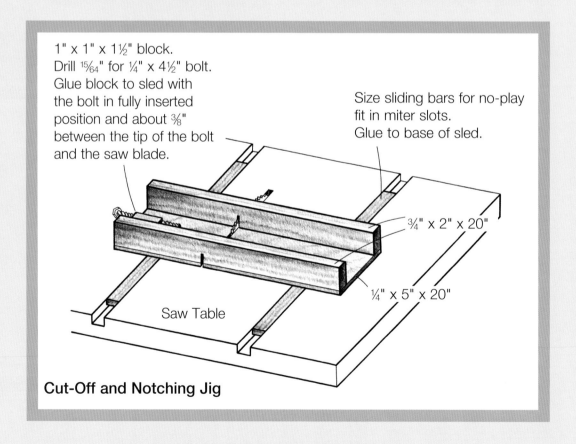

1" x 1" x 1½" block.
Drill ¹⁵⁄₆₄" for ¼" x 4½" bolt.
Glue block to sled with the bolt in fully inserted position and about ⅜" between the tip of the bolt and the saw blade.

Size sliding bars for no-play fit in miter slots.
Glue to base of sled.

¾" x 2" x 20"

¼" x 5" x 20"

Saw Table

Cut-Off and Notching Jig

fence. When the glue sets, adjust the saw blade to cut a little more than ¼ inch and run the jig through.

For the jig option shown below left, prepare a block about 1x1x2 inches and drill a ¹⁵⁄₆₄-inch hole down the center of the long axis. Insert a ¼ x 4½-inch bolt into this hole—the bolt will form its own threads in the block. With the bolt screwed all the way in, glue the block so that there is about a 2½-inch gap between the head of the bolt and the saw kerf running across the bottom of the sled.

By using a caliper, the gage blocks, and trial-and-error with scrap material, the setting of the screw stop can be made with great accuracy prior to making cuts in the puzzle pieces.

Extending this jig a little on the left end and adding a hold-down clamp as shown below will enable it to be used safely and accurately to cut off small parts such as those needed for the *Pocoloco* and *Fifth Avenue* puzzles.

Hold-Down Clamp Options

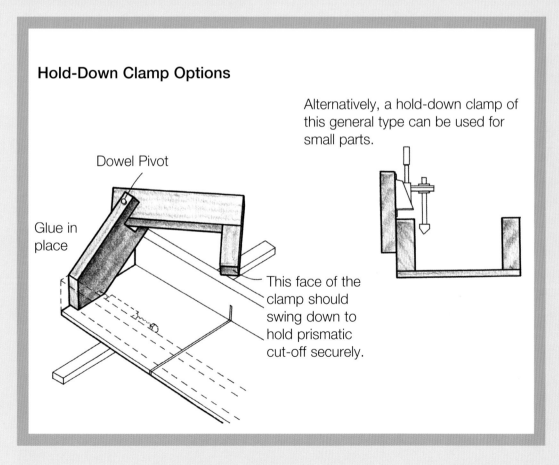

Dowel Pivot

Glue in place

Alternatively, a hold-down clamp of this general type can be used for small parts.

This face of the clamp should swing down to hold prismatic cut-off securely.

Figure 77—The Level 5 Notchable Six-Piece Burr, *assembled (above) and taken apart (below).*

Chapter 10

Level 5 Notchable Six-Piece Burr

Designed by Bill Cutler

There are burr puzzles and then there are burr puzzles (**Figure 77**). Bill Cutler has done extensive computer analysis of the family of six-piece burrs, and in 1987 he discovered this unique design. "Level 5" refers to the smallest number of moves needed to remove the first piece from the assembled puzzle. In the most common six-piece burrs, the first piece to be removed has no notches and is simply pushed straight out. "Notchable" means all the pieces can be made by cutting one or more simple notches. An un-notchable piece could not be completely cut on a table saw (**Figure 78**). What makes this puzzle unique is that it is the highest possible level notchable six-piece burr, and it has only one solution. It is also a difficult puzzle to solve. But that doesn't mean it is a difficult puzzle to make.

All of the pieces of this puzzle could be simply cut on a table saw by measuring, marking-out, and aligning each cut with the saw blade. However, greater accuracy, repeatability, and speed can be achieved if you take the trouble to make a simple jig and a few gage blocks (see *Cut-Off and Notching Jig*, page 66). Cutting the

notches can be done with a dado head on your saw, but multiple passes with a general purpose blade will go swiftly enough, especially if you are making only one of these puzzles.

Begin by preparing 3 feet of 1 x 1-inch square stock, utilizing any well-behaved hardwood you may have around the shop (see *Making a Square Stick,* page 18). Cut one end square, and then cut three pieces 6½ inches long—each of these three pieces will make two puzzle parts. Cutting the notches in these 6½-inch pieces and flipping them end-for-end in the cutting sequence gives you something more to hold on to than you would have working with 3-inch pieces. Further, it ensures that you are always referencing each cut from the same end of the piece, minimizing error. The two 3-inch pieces will be cut apart after the notching has been done. Note that parts E and F are identical. The rest of the stick will be used for making gage blocks, trial cuts as you set up the end stops, and for spare material if you make a mistake. (Who, me?)

Ideally, the fit of all parts of this puzzle into all notches would be perfect—no slop, no force

Figure 78—Typical Burr Pieces

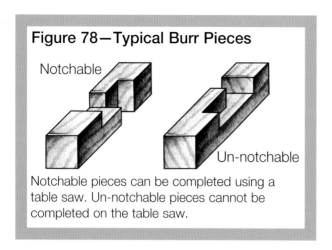

Notchable

Un-notchable

Notchable pieces can be completed using a table saw. Un-notchable pieces cannot be completed on the table saw.

Figure 79—Gage Blocks

If the burr pieces are not exactly 1" x 1", adjust the lengths of these gage blocks accordingly.

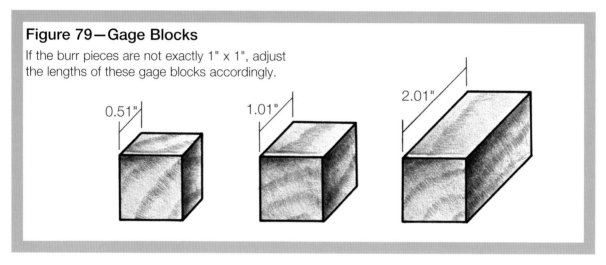

0.51"

1.01"

2.01"

Figure 80
Setting Depth of Cut

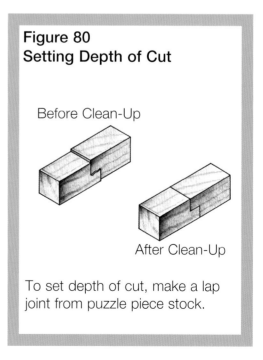

Before Clean-Up

After Clean-Up

To set depth of cut, make a lap joint from puzzle piece stock.

required. For your first attempt, at least, opening up the tolerances just a bit is advised, enabling the parts to go together easily. The puzzle is difficult enough without mechanical binding. It is not like the *Bi-Burr* or the *Pocoloco* puzzles where the fit has to be exact or the puzzle really doesn't work. The *Level 5 Notchable* is a great puzzle even if the parts fit a bit loosely. The problem is that, as the assembly of the puzzle builds, as each additional part is added, small dimensional errors can accumulate, potentially making the last moves in the assembly too difficult, requiring too much force. So, try for a fit that is one- or two-pieces-of-paper loose. Cut three gage blocks from the leftover 1 x 1-inch stick; one that is one-half the width of the stick, one that is the full width of the stick, and one that is twice as long as the width of the stick (**Figure 79**). The gage blocks should all be oversize by about 0.01 inch. Use a micrometer or vernier caliper to get these gages just right.

Set the saw blade to cut half-way through the puzzle parts, taking into account the thickness of the jig base. You will want to clean up the bottoms of the notches later, using a chisel and/or file, so the saw cut shouldn't go quite half way. Use a vernier caliper or make a test lap joint from two short lengths of the extra stick to get the depth of cut spot on (**Figure 80**). This saw blade depth setting will be used for all of the notches.

Place the notching jig on the table saw with the slide bars in the slots, and run the jig through the blade. Using a scrap stick, adjust the screw stop so that it is one inch from the blade. With one of the 6½-inch workpieces up against the end of the bolt, **Figure 81**, make the first cut—this will become piece A in **Figure 82**. Lightly pencil in the letters A through F on the ends of the sticks for easy reference as you cut the notches. Reposition the screw stop to make a cut ½ inch from the blade, and make a cut in the other end of this stick and at both ends of the other two sticks. Now, back the stop screw away from the blade by a little less than the thickness of the blade and cut again in what will become pieces B through F. Continue to readjust the stop and widen the notches, following the drawings in **Figure 82**.

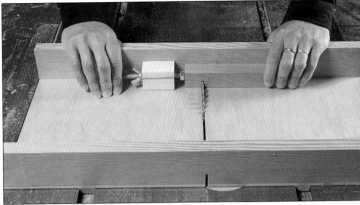

Figure 81—Saw the first cut using the notching jig. Note that if a jig of this type were to be used for through cut-offs, a device to hold the cut-offs in place would be required.

As you approach a ½-inch notch width, make the adjustments slowly and carefully, trying the ½-inch gage block with each pass. You are trying to obtain a snug fit of the gage into the notches on pieces C and D. When the gage block just fits in with light finger pressure, those notches will be finished.

After these narrow notches in pieces C and D are complete, leave the gage block partly in the notch and adjust the stop screw so that the saw blade just scrapes against the gage. This will be the proper setting for the first cut in the middle notch in these pieces. Of course, the sticks will have to be rolled 90 degrees when you begin to cut this middle notch. By now, you get the idea—reset the screw stop, cut, gage, roll the stick, and repeat. Continue these operations until you have completed all the notches on all six pieces. You have only to cut off the six pieces to length, 3 inches, clean up the bottom of the notches and any other roughness, and assemble the puzzle.

Ah, yes, assemble the puzzle. The assembly steps are shown in **Figure 84**. You may want to try to put the puzzle together on your own, without looking at the figure, but be warned that it is quite difficult. Disassembly requires the same steps in the reverse order. When complete, put it on a shelf as a trophy for your tenacity, or give it as a gift to your mean boss.

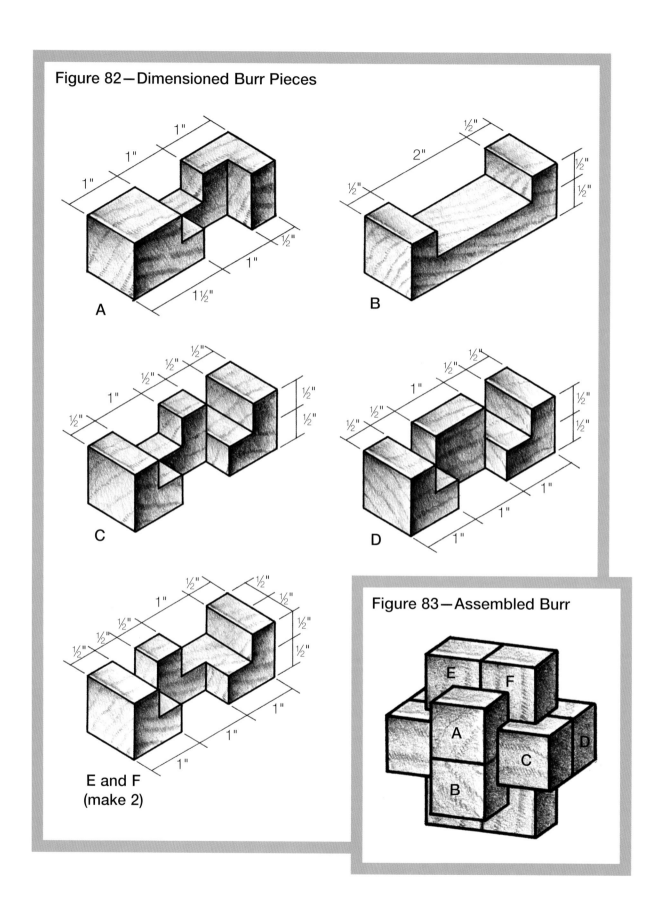

Figure 82—Dimensioned Burr Pieces

A

B

C

D

E and F
(make 2)

Figure 83—Assembled Burr

Figure 84—Assembling the *Level 5 Notchable 6-Piece Burr*

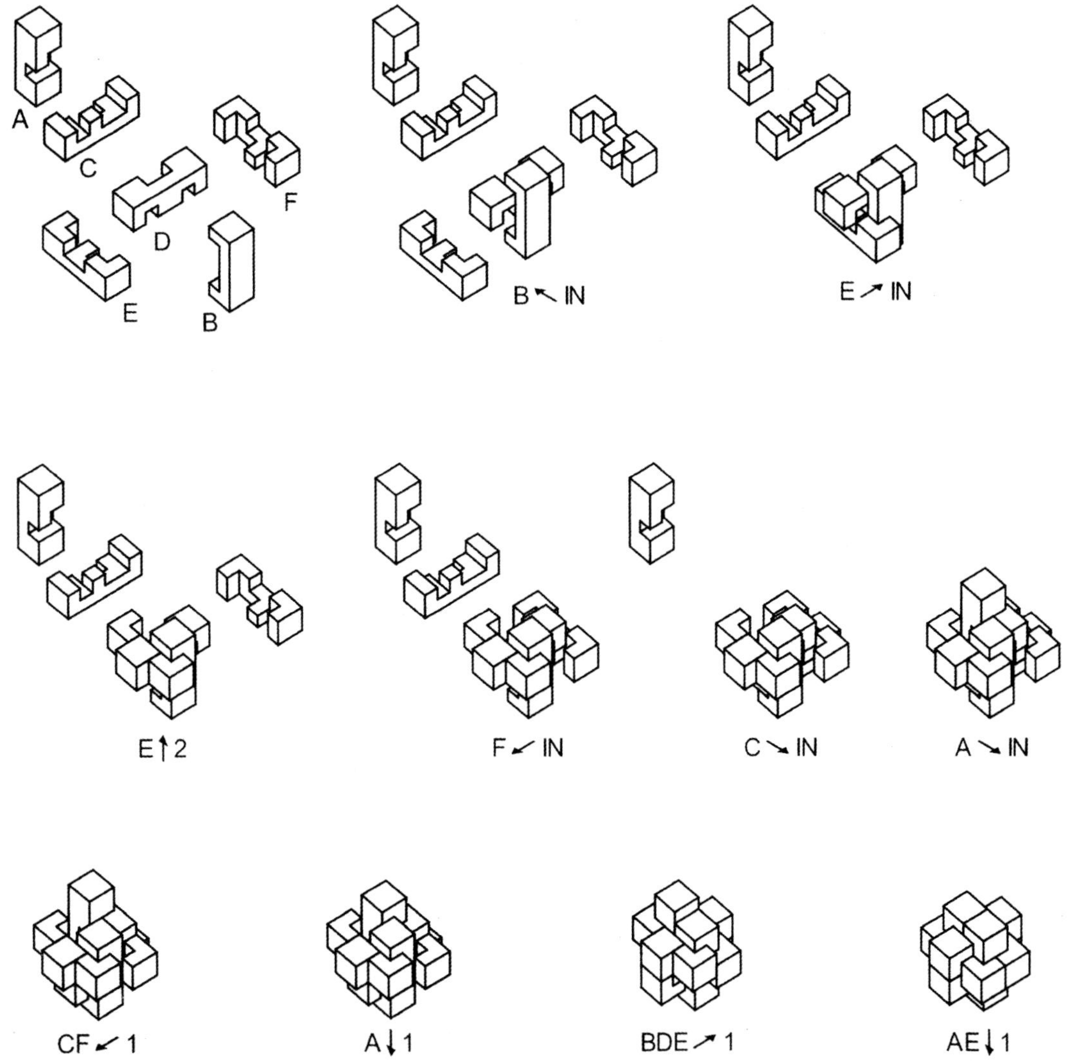

A

C

E B

D

F

B ⭦ IN

E ⭧ IN

E ↑ 2

F ⭦ IN

C ⭨ IN

A ⭨ IN

CF ⭩ 1

A ↓ 1

BDE ⭧ 1

AE ↓ 1

Figure 85—Pandora's Box, *assembled and disassembled*

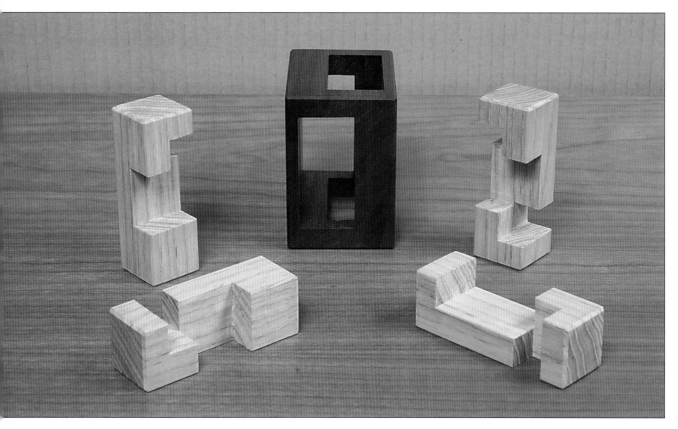

Chapter 11

Pandora's Box

Designed by Brian Young

In the puzzle world, *Pandora's Box* is referred to as a "boxed burr." The four puzzle pieces are notched in a manner typical of any burr puzzle, but the difference is that they must be assembled within a cage or box, adding significantly to the difficulty of finding the solution. The four pieces must be inserted into the box in the correct orientation and order, without the solver being able to fully see the progression of moves.

Although the notch patterns and dimensions are not the same as those of the puzzle pieces in the *Level 5 Notchable Six Piece Burr* (**page 68**), the same basic cutting techniques can be employed—preparing the square stick, setting up an adjustable stop on your saw, etc. As with the other puzzles, any seasoned hardwood will do, though contrasting species for the burr pieces and box will add to the visual appeal of the final product. Using the dimensions shown in **Figure 86** and the suggestions given for constructing the *Level 5 Burr*, make the four burr pieces for *Pandora's Box*. Because the assembly process for solving the puzzle is essentially blind, a very slightly looser fit of the parts would be advised. This clearance, about 0.005 inch or the thickness of a piece of paper, can be achieved by either making the square stick a tiny bit smaller than the nominal one inch dimension or by lightly sanding the four finished puzzle pieces later.

The box can be made from one piece of wood, but it may be somewhat difficult to do a clean job of the through mortises. Instead, make the bottom and top halves as shown in **Figure 87**, using a table mounted router or table saw, and glue them together at the corner posts. Note that although the top and bottom halves are dimensionally the same, one part should be cut with the grain at right angles to the other so that when they are glued together, the grain in the two parts will be running in the same direction. Using the dimensions shown, the burr pieces will extend a little beyond flush with the sides of the box. Although having the pieces stand a bit proud of the box sides is primarily a decorative feature, it also helps to mask the slight looseness in the internal joints when the puzzle is assembled.

The solution to the puzzle involves a minimum of twelve steps. Normally, a puzzle like this would be sitting around in the assembled state, waiting for someone to pick it up and start playing with it—*disassembly* first. But, since you will be making the pieces, your first job will be *assembly*—a somewhat more difficult task. The solution described here will help you put the pieces together. Disassembly involves the same moves but in reverse order. Note that in the assembled, or solved, state, piece C is the only one that will move, so even though you will not

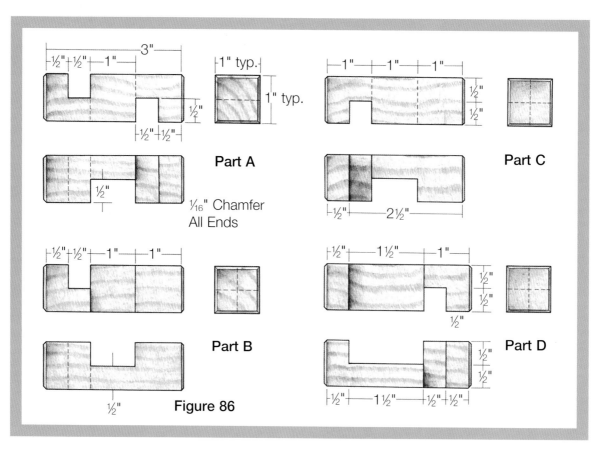

Part A

¹⁄₁₆" Chamfer
All Ends

Part B

Part C

Part D

Figure 86

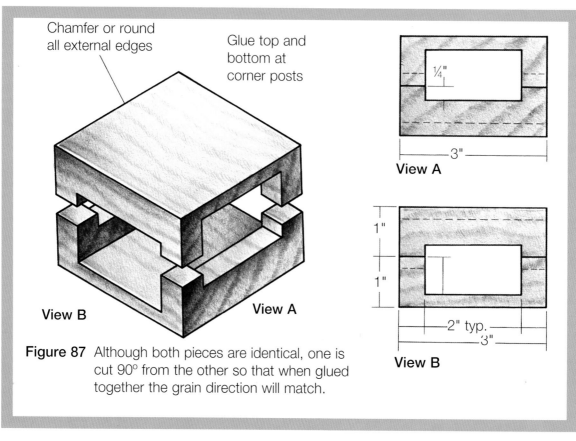

Chamfer or round
all external edges

Glue top and
bottom at
corner posts

View A

View B

View A

View B

Figure 87 Although both pieces are identical, one is
cut 90° from the other so that when glued
together the grain direction will match.

be able to identify the pieces from their hidden notch patterns, you should be able to find piece C and orient the puzzle with the solution diagram.

Lay out the four burr pieces and the box as shown in **Figure 88**. It may help to fix a small piece of masking tape to the ends of the pieces and write the letters A through D on their ends. Now, make the moves listed in **Figure 88**.

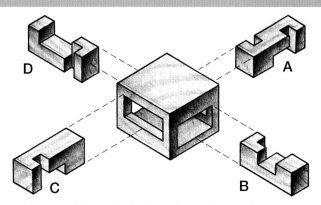

Figure 88— Solution Start Position

Assembling *Pandora's Box*

- Slide piece A in leaving it ½ inch short—out of the box.

- Slide piece B in under piece A and ½ inch past and out of the box on the other side.

- Slide piece C in over piece B and next to piece A leaving it ½ inch short—out of the box.

- Slide piece D in under piece C and next to piece B leaving it 1½ inches short—out of the box.

- Slide piece C in a further ½ inch–it should now be flush inside the box.

- Slide piece B in a further ½ inch–it should now be flush inside the box.

- Slide piece A in a further ½ inch–it should now be flush inside the box.

- Slide piece D in a further ½ inch–it should now be 1 inch outside the box.

- Slide piece C ½ inch back out of the box.

- Slide piece B ½ inch back out of the box—be careful, it will slide farther.

- Slide piece A ½ inch back out of the box.

- Slide piece D a further 1 inch–it should now be flush inside the box.

- Slide piece A, then piece B, then piece C each ½ inch back inside the box.

Figure 89—*Assembled* Pegasus—*coming and going*

Chapter 12

Pegasus

Designed by Tad Muroi

Presented with the assembled puzzle, **Figure 89**, the solver will encounter only modest difficulty in disassembling and reassembling the three parts of *Pegasus*. Each of the three parts is in itself a glued together subassembly of four separate pieces (**Figures 92** through **96**). Although this puzzle is a three-part geometric puzzle, it is disguised as a charming mythical figure.

All twelve elemental pieces of this puzzle can be cut from a plank of ½-inch stock—black walnut would be a good choice, though virtually any stable (pun recognized and not avoided) species will work well. Begin by preparing enough wood for all 12 puzzle pieces, about 5½ x 15 x ½ inches. At this stage, it is most important that the thickness is uniform and the surface quality be flat, smooth, and free of tool marks. Make copies of the full-size drawings in **Figure 90** and **91** and, using a spray adhesive, glue the copy to the blank.

Tadao Muroi

Tadao Muroi (1921-2000) graduated in engineering from the Yokohama National University. He became a physics teacher at Tokyo Metropolitan High School. Mr. Muroi was a puzzle designer and member of the Academy of Recreational Mathematics, Japan.

Although other tools and methods can be employed, the scroll saw is the best tool for cutting out the twelve pieces. A band saw with a fine blade or even a coping saw could be used instead, but you would need to do more clean-up of all sawn edges for a good looking final result. To assure that all parts fit together just right, while cutting out the pieces, give special care to the six ½-inch wide notches in pieces A, B, and C. When you are finished cutting out and cleaning these notches, they should snugly accommodate the ½-inch thickness of the stock. This fit must be just a bit tight after the paper pattern has been peeled off and the parts have been lightly sanded.

Drill a ⅛-inch hole about ⅛ inch deep on each side of the head on part A to create the eyes.

No matter how careful you are in cutting out the pieces, it is likely that some edge clean-up will be required. At this point, attend only to those edges that fit against other parts—either glued or sliding. Clean up these edges to make neat joints. Study the photographs of the assembled puzzle and note the pieces that form the body. Some of the outside edges of these pieces can be cleaned up more accurately if you wait until the parts have been glued together and you can better see where excess material should be removed.

Figure 90—
Pegasus **Pattern**

★ These slots
must snugly fit
the ½" wood

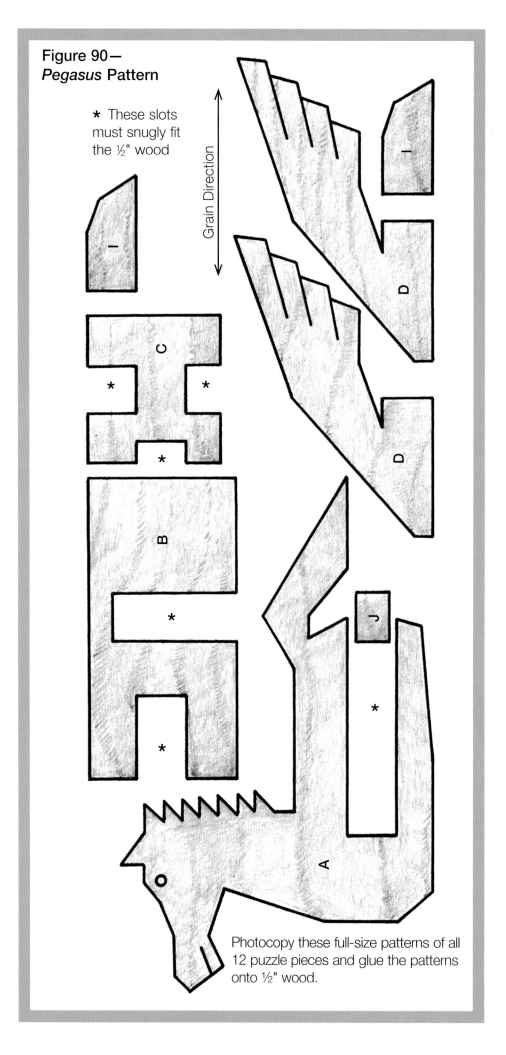

Grain Direction

Photocopy these full-size patterns of all
12 puzzle pieces and glue the patterns
onto ½" wood.

80

Although each of the three subassemblies can be glued together directly as shown in **Figures 92 through 96,** you will achieve better results and tighter joints by constructing the CDJ subassembly (glue on I later) in **Figure 92**, and then continuing to add parts in the sequence indicated.

Glue the small piece, J, to part C as shown in **Figure 92**. Now, glue the left wing, part D, to part C, as shown in the same figure. Assemble, without glue, part B with the CDJ subassembly, **Figure 93**, and slide this build-up into the long notch in part A as shown in **Figure 94**. When in place, the front of A and B should line up flush to form the chest. Now you can glue on the legs, parts E, F, G, and H, the right wing, D, and the two haunch pieces, I, using the photographs and illustrations as a guide for where to apply the glue. Be very careful not to have any excess glue inadvertently squeeze out and cement the subassemblies together!

Before the glue completely sets up, gently slide the three subassemblies apart to be certain that they are not frozen together. The first step in disassembly is accomplished by holding the front legs, (Assembly Three, **Figure 96**), in one hand, the rear legs, (actually, subassemblies One and Two as shown in **Figures 92** and **93**) in the other, and pulling apart; then separate subassembly One and subassembly Two. See **Figures 97, 98** and **99**. After the glue fully sets, clean up the assembled puzzle by sanding each side on a sheet of sandpaper taped to a flat surface so that all parts are flush and even. With a sharp chisel and sandpaper, clean up the edges of all remaining body parts. Finish the puzzle by applying a penetrating oil.

Although *Pegasus* may not be the most difficult puzzle to solve in this collection, it is likely to pose a few construction challenges as you attempt to use the scroll saw to produce straight and accurate cuts.

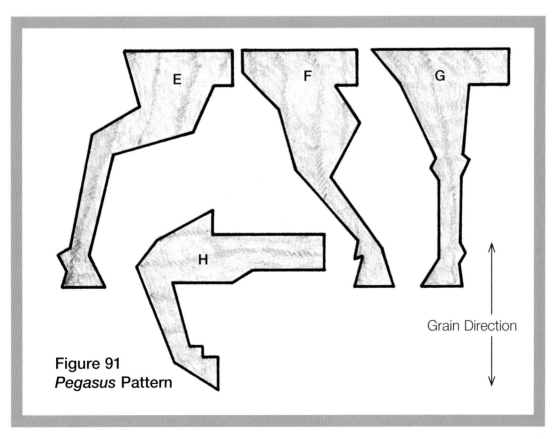

Figure 91
Pegasus Pattern

Grain Direction

Figure 92—Subassembly One

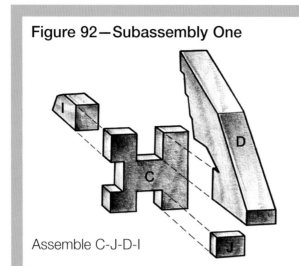

Assemble C-J-D-I

Figure 93

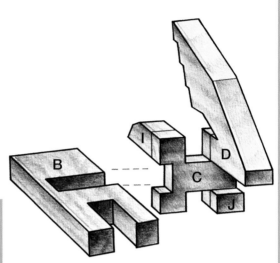

Fit CJDI into B. B is not glued to CJDI subassembly; it is used here only to facilitate alignment of parts.

Figure 94

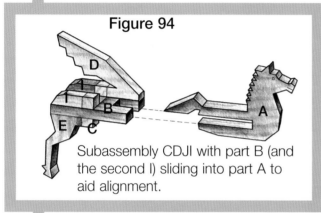

Subassembly CDJI with part B (and the second I) sliding into part A to aid alignment.

Figure 95—Subassembly Two

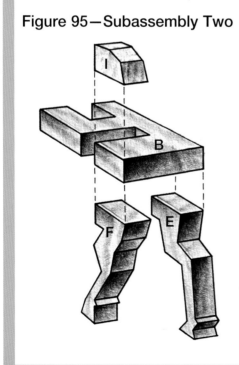

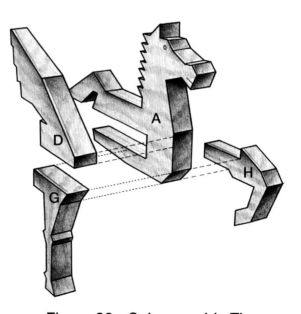

Figure 96—Subassembly Three

Figue 97—*Assembled* Pegasus *in the hands of someone beginning to disassemble the puzzle.*

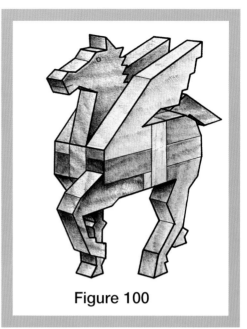

Figure 100

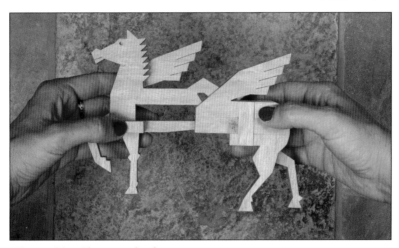

Figure 98—*Showing the first step in disassembling the puzzle.*

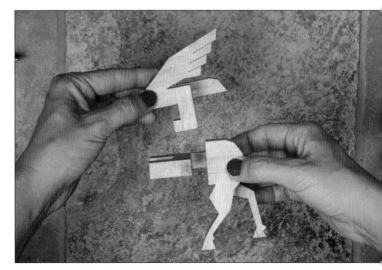

Figure 99—*Showing the second, (last), step in disassembling the puzzle.*

Figure 101—*The mysterious Celt.*

Chapter 13

The Celt

Designed by Og, the Stone-Age Toolmaker

Behold the mysterious Celt,

With a property that confuses.

One way it will spin,

The other it refuses.

The Celt is not really a puzzle, and it clearly is not a contemporary invention, but it certainly qualifies as a puzzling object (**Figure 101**). When placed on a smooth, hard, flat surface, such as a glass top table or granite kitchen counter, and then rotated with a flick of a finger, *The Celt* will spin freely and smoothly in one direction, but not the other. In fact, if spun in the direction it does not want to go, it will immediately start to rock and rattle and turn itself around to spin in the preferred direction. Why it behaves so peculiarly is understood by some physicists and mathematicians who have analyzed it, but it should suffice for present purposes to say that *The Celt's* strange motion is a result of a subtle asymmetry that is built into its shape—not aerodynamics, not magnetism, not the Coriolis effect.

This phenomenon was really discovered, not invented. It resulted from a not-quite successful attempt at symmetry. More than 100 years ago, a paleontologist was idly playing with a stone chopping implement (a "celt" after the Latin "celtis" or chopping tool), estimated to be about 50,000 years old. He observed, while spinning

it on his desk, that it had a strange dynamic property—it spun smoothly clockwise, but not counterclockwise. Intrigued, he brought the relic to a colleague, a mathematician named G. T. Walker, for analysis. Walker discovered the asymmetry that was responsible for its odd spinning behavior and published his findings in the *British Quarterly of Mathematics* in 1896. Since that time, *The Celt*, sometimes renamed as Wobblestone or Rattleback, has appeared in a number of books, magazine articles, and journals. In recent times, celts have been produced commercially in plastic and aluminum. The word "celt," by the way, is pronounced "selt."

Making *The Celt* of wood is not very difficult, but some experimentation and iteration will be required. Most of the work is performed with abrasive tools and materials, making this project decidedly different from the others in this book. The work is basically all done free-hand, but do not be concerned about the difficulty of obtaining some precise mathematically determined contour—there are an infinite number of contours that will work, each a bit different from all the rest, all similar and all interesting. Study the diagrams and remember that the contour of the bottom must be very smooth and free of flat spots, especially where *The Celt* contacts the table.

The shape you are trying to achieve on the bottom

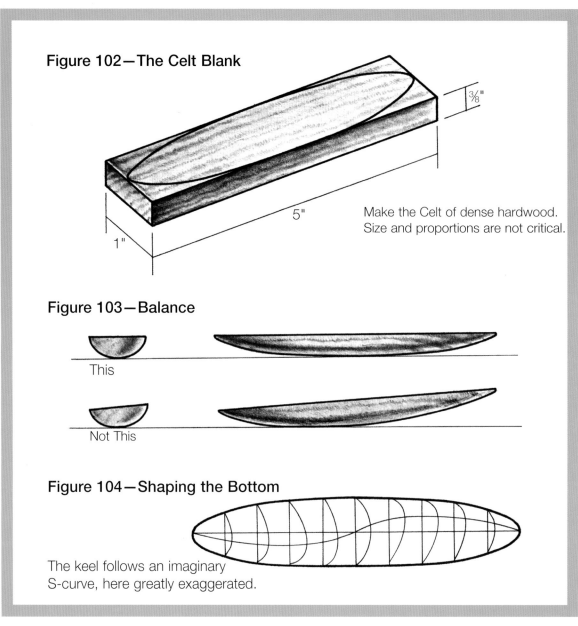

Figure 102—The Celt Blank

3/8"

5"

1"

Make the Celt of dense hardwood.
Size and proportions are not critical.

Figure 103—Balance

This

Not This

Figure 104—Shaping the Bottom

The keel follows an imaginary
S-curve, here greatly exaggerated.

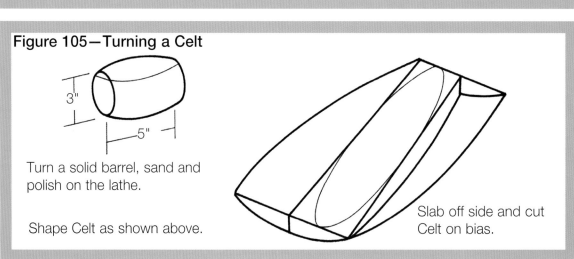

Figure 105—Turning a Celt

3"

5"

Turn a solid barrel, sand and
polish on the lathe.

Shape Celt as shown above.

Slab off side and cut
Celt on bias.

of *The Celt* is somewhat propeller like, but far more subtle. If you were to imagine that this is the hull of a ship, the keel, instead of lying along a straight line, would be distorted into a slight S shape. In practice, one attempts to make the shape symmetrical, and then deliberately upsets the symmetry by very slightly flattening opposite quadrants. After this, the piece is carefully sanded and polished.

Begin with a piece of dense hardwood—perhaps ebony, rosewood, lignum vitae, or snakewood—measuring about 5 inches long, ⅜ inch thick, and 1 inch wide. Larger, smaller, or differently proportioned pieces would work as well, but this size is a good place to start. Flatten and smooth one 5 x 1-inch surface. Draw or trace the outline of a symmetrical elongated oval on the piece, **Figure 102**, and cut to that shape using a band saw, coping saw, or simply create the shape on a disk sander (**Figures 106** and **107**). Now, using a rasp, files, a scraper, a disk or stationary belt sander, and hand-held sandpaper, **Figure 108**, shape the underside of *The Celt* to look like **Figure 104**. It should be symmetrical in appearance, both from end-to-end as well as from side-to-side. Place it on a table and check that it rests with its top flat surface parallel to the table, neither tipping to one side nor to one end (**Figure 103**). Correct any imbalance or lopsidedness and check again. Smooth the contour through different grades of sandpaper, trying to achieve a very fair surface, free of bumps, flats, or irregularities. Check again on the table.

At this point, you may have already created *The Celt*. Try to spin it both clockwise and counterclockwise. Does it spin freely in one direction? If not, you may not have achieved an adequately smooth contour. Does it reverse itself and spin in the other direction? If not, you may have been too successful in your attempt at symmetry. Carefully flatten opposite quadrants of the bottom, just a little at a time, as shown in **Figure 104**, smooth the surface, and test again. This iterative process is necessary because *The Celt*, even if shaped correctly, will not perform well if it and the table are not extremely smooth and clean. This fact

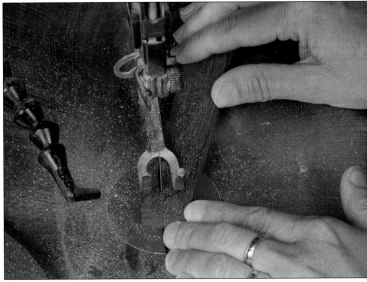

Figure 106—Cut the body of the Celt using a scroll saw or band saw.

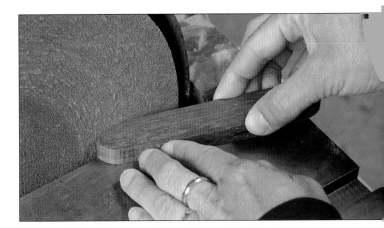

Figure 107—Clean up the contour of the blank using a disk sander.

Figure 108—Shape the back of the Celt with files and rasps.

Figure 109—The belt sander makes short work of contouring the back of the Celt.

Figure 110—Polish the surface by hand-sanding.

has the opposite quadrants slightly flattened like a left-handed rather than right-handed propeller, will exhibit the opposite behavior, reversing itself clockwise to counterclockwise, instead of counterclockwise to clockwise, or visa versa. Perhaps this is a clue as to whether the Neolithic toolmaker was right or left-handed. Smaller celts rattle at higher frequencies and larger celts exhibit a more lumbering, slower behavior.

A slightly different form of celt can be made using a lathe. Turn and polish a barrel shape as shown in **Figure 105**. Next, cut a ⅜-inch slab off the side of the barrel. Now, cut out the elliptical shape from the slab as shown and contour the piece to taste, taking care not to upset the balance or alter the surface where it meets the table. Check out the reversing action and fine-tune the balance as needed.

To avoid the difficulty of holding and slicing off the slab, you might wish to make the barrel blank by gluing two pieces at the cut line. The slab can be easily split off after turning if you sandwich a piece of brown wrapping paper at the glue line. This method has several advantages: the barrel can be used over and over again should you wish to make more than one celt, and the glued-on piece from which *The Celt* will be made can be fastened at an angle so that in the finished piece the grain will line up with its long axis.

The Celt is more than just a fun plaything to fondle and spin. Legend has it that a prehistoric tribe used *The Celt* as a directional compass, calling it a "tates." The high priest would spin the tates on his stone altar, noting the direction it was pointing when it stopped spinning. As you might expect, it would come to rest pointing in a different and arbitrary direction every time. The tates was obviously not very useful as a compass, but the unsuccessful attempt by this primitive tribe to harness a natural phenomenon did give rise to a common adage in use even today—"He who has a tates is lost."

gives rise to an interesting paradox—would *The Celt* work on an ideal, frictionless surface? If so, what is it pushing against as it reverses itself? The asymmetry that you are trying to achieve should be barely detectable. When you are happy with the looks, feel and performance of *The Celt*, ease or chamfer the sharp edges, apply a bit of oil or wax, and amaze your friends.

Additional experimentation will alter the liveliness of *The Celt*, affect how long it continues to spin after it reverses itself, and might even produce a shape that reverses itself multiple times. As you might guess, a mirror-image *Celt*, one that

Adapted from an article by Allan Boardman, "The Mysterious Celt," published in the July/August 1983 issue of *Fine Woodworking* magazine.

Chapter 14

Fritz the Wonder Dog

Designed by Jack Botermans

Fritz has real personality and to lots of people, this is what a mechanical puzzle should be—he is fun to look at and play with, appeals to people of all ages at first sight, and is not overly difficult to solve (**Figure 115,** page 92). Upon picking up a puzzle, many solvers want and expect to find a key piece and/or a key move to begin the disassembly; *Fritz* has both a key move and a key piece. They want to maintain a clear mental image of what the puzzle is supposed to look like when they start to reassemble the pile of pieces; it's hard to forget what this little pooch looks like. And they really want the pieces to offer visual clues to where they go in the reassembly process; one can't mistake the headpiece for the hind legs, nor be confused about which end they should be on! Expect this puzzle to be played with a lot.

In making *Fritz* you will find that all of the pieces have different shapes and cutting them out will

Jack Botermans

Jack Botermans (b. 1949) studied mechanical engineering, art, and design in the Netherlands. He graduated with distinction in 1973.

He has been a free-lance designer since 1986, specializing in three-dimensional designs for exhibitions and in games and puzzles. As a designer and writer he has published over 50 books on many subjects, amongst which are various works on games and puzzles. He has received a number of awards for his work in both Europe and the United States.

He currently owns a company that produces puzzles for retail sales. He continues to write and is working on books concerned with nostalgic subjects, hobby books, and another puzzle book with Jerry Slocum of Beverly Hills, California. Mr. Botermans lives in France.

Figure 112—*Fritz's* Anatomy

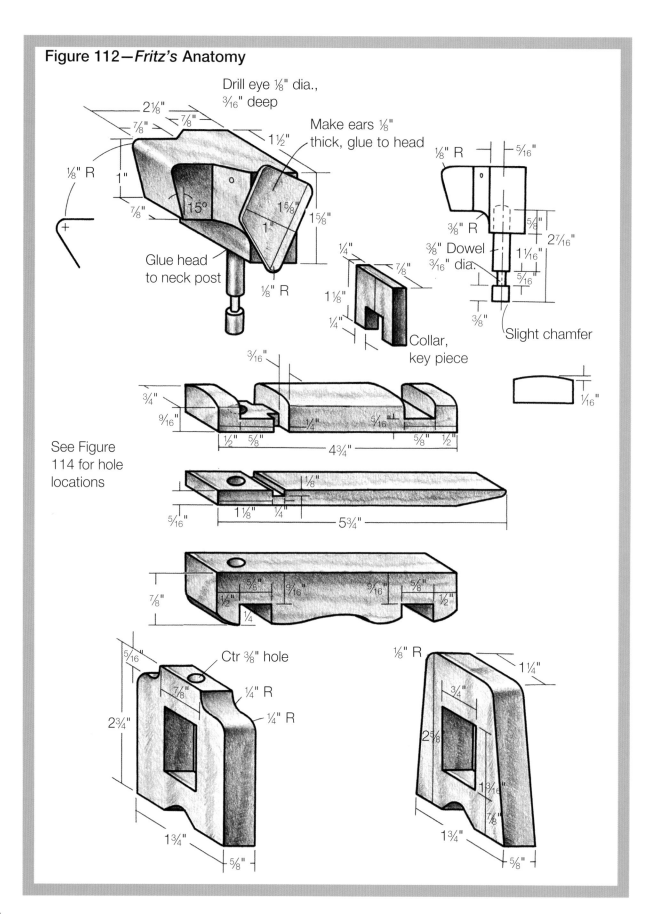

Drill eye ⅛" dia., ³⁄₁₆" deep

Make ears ⅛" thick, glue to head

2⅛"
⅞"
⅞"
1½"
⅛" R
1"
⅞"
15°
1⅝"
1"
1⅝"
⅛" R

Glue head to neck post

⅛" R
⅜" R
⅜" Dowel ³⁄₁₆" dia.
⅛" R
⁵⁄₁₆"
⅝"
2⁷⁄₁₆"
1¹⁄₁₆"
⁵⁄₁₆"
⅜"
Slight chamfer

¼"
⅞"
1⅛"
¼"

Collar, key piece

³⁄₁₆"
¾"
⁹⁄₁₆"
½" ⅝"
¼"
⁵⁄₁₆"
⅝" ½"
4¾"

1⁄₁₆"

See Figure 114 for hole locations

⅛"
1⅛" ¼"
⁵⁄₁₆"
5¾"

⅞"
½"
⅝"
⁹⁄₁₆"
¼"
⁹⁄₁₆"
⅝" ½"

⁵⁄₁₆"
Ctr ⅜" hole
⅞"
¼" R
¼" R
2¾"
1¾"
⅝"

⅛" R
1¼"
¾"
2⅝"
1³⁄₁₆"
⅞"
1¾"
⅝"

require a variety of set-ups. But, where you can, take advantage of the commonalities. For instance, when making the three body parts (**Figure 112**), most of the notching can be done with the same end-stop settings on your saw.

Any available domestic hardwood will do; try to find some dogwood if you can, or use two or more different species for contrast and interest. The dimensions of the head may require you to glue two pieces together, but all other parts can be made using commonly available stock. Start by making the three body parts, **Figure 112**. Using a bench plane or thickness planer, prepare a piece of stock ¾ inch thick with smooth, parallel faces, large enough to make all three parts. If the wood you have selected has any significant figure or grain pattern, you may want to cut out the three parts such that when the puzzle is assembled, the pattern is preserved. Rounding of the upper part, contouring the lower part, and shaping the tail can wait until after the joints have been cut and fit. Cut all the ⅝-inch notches and the other details at the front end of the upper part following the plan in **Figure 112**. To simplify cutting the notches accurately, you may wish to devise and use a jig similar to the one described on page 66.

The front and hind leg pieces have rectangular window cutouts. To avoid the difficulty of

Figure 113—Both halves of each leg piece, already notched, are ready to be glued.

drilling/chiseling out these openings, make and glue together two identical halves for each of these pieces (**Figure 113**). Before gluing the halves together, test to be sure that the openings fit the body parts. The outlines of the leg parts can be cut later. After gluing, assemble the body and leg parts, and check to see that *Fritz* is stable on all fours. At the top center of the front leg part, mark the location for the drilled ⅜-inch hole, and drill through all four pieces, noting that the center body part must be positioned ³⁄₃₂ inch to the rear (**Figure 114**). Be very careful to drill the hole in the exact center of the assembly. Any drilling inaccuracy or asymmetry will prevent assembly if the leg piece were flipped over.

Figure 114—Drilling the Holes

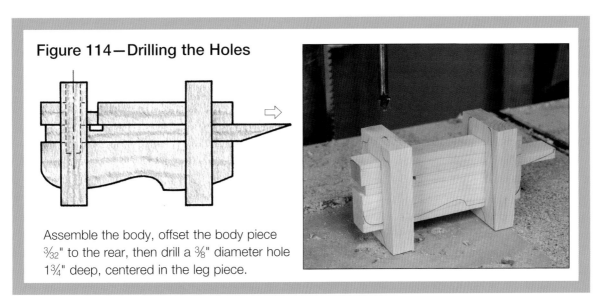

Assemble the body, offset the body piece ³⁄₃₂" to the rear, then drill a ⅜" diameter hole 1¾" deep, centered in the leg piece.

Figure 115—Fritz, *assembled*

Puzzle Projects for Woodworkers

Snug fits are not required in this puzzle since all the pieces lock together—the parts want to fit with a pleasant but controlled looseness. A sheet of paper should just slip between mating parts when the puzzle is fully assembled. The single exception is the collar. Since this is the key piece, it should slide into place with a slight amount of friction so that it doesn't fall out unintentionally and give away the secret of disassembly.

The cuts required to make the head can be made on a band saw and cleaned up with a file and sandpaper. Drill the ⅜-inch hole for the neck post and the ⅛-inch holes for the eyes, as shown in **Figure 112**. The notch on the neck post can be turned on a lathe, or made by filing the ⅜-inch dowel while it is chucked in a vise-mounted electric drill or drill press. While you are at it, sand the diameter of the dowel to just under ⅜ inch for an easy fit in the drilled hole, and cut a slight chamfer on the free end. Glue the neck post into the head, making sure that the notch in the post is positioned to engage with the center body part.

Prepare a ⅛-inch piece of wood for the ears, shape them with a disc sander, and glue them to the head. When you are satisfied that all pieces fit together properly, cut the curved underside of *Fritz's* belly piece on a band or scroll saw. Clean up the cut with a drum sander, shape the leg pieces, round over the top body part, and lightly ease all sharp edges on each piece.

The secret to solving this puzzle, although obvious by now, involves rotating *Fritz's* head (the key move) so that he is looking backwards (**Figure 116**). It is now possible to raise the collar (the key piece), allowing the center body part to slide ³⁄₃₂ inch rearward. With this move, the head can be taken off and the other parts disassembled. Break out the kibble and enjoy your new house pet!

Adapted from an article by Allan Boardman, "Fritz the Wonder Dog," published in the December 1990 issue of *American Woodworker* magazine.

Figure 116—Solving the Puzzle

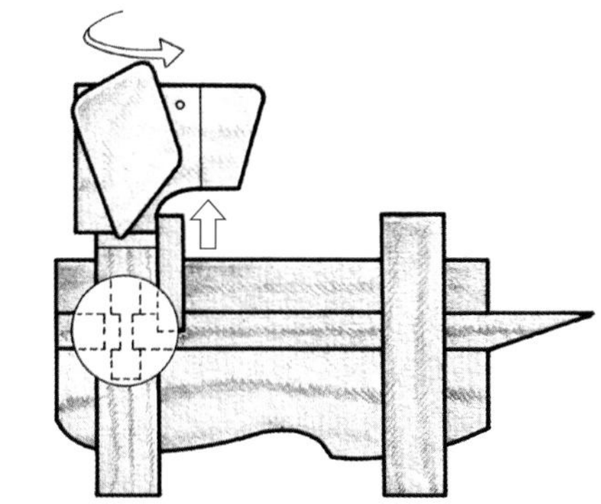

Step 1. Turn the head to face the rear. Lift the collar.

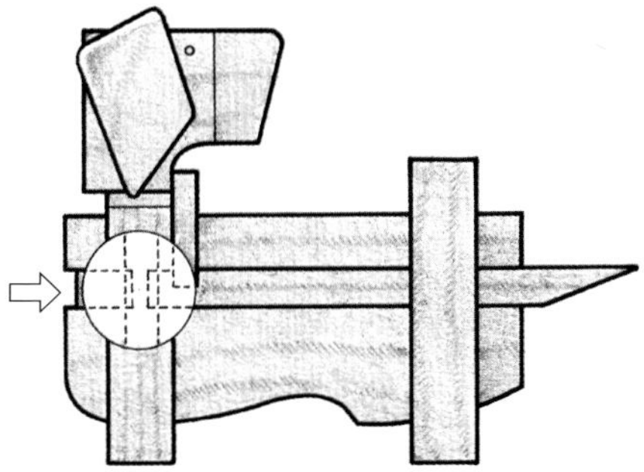

Step 2. Move the body center piece slightly to the rear.

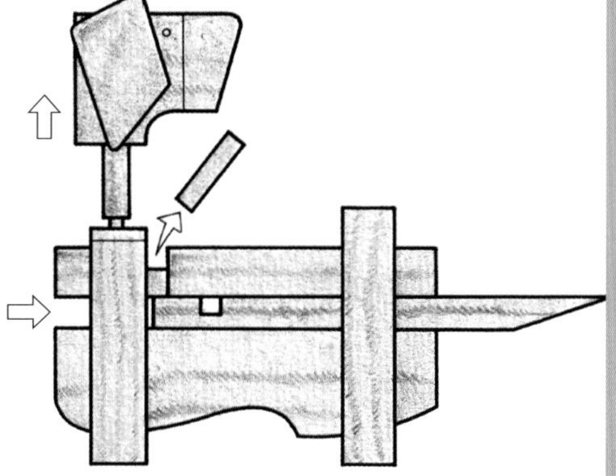

Step 3. Lift the head and collar off, then remove the center piece.

Imperial to Metric Conversion

All project dimensions in this book are presented using the Imperial (American) measurement system, inches and fractions thereof. While it is recognized that many woodworkers are more accustomed to working in the Metric system, conversion from Imperial to Metric is usually messy and, especially when tight tolerances are needed, often involves carrying a number of decimal places for precise representation.

Coping with this awkward problem can be off-putting. I believe that the most practical solution is for the Metric woodworker to acquire a few basic Imperial measurement tools, a ruler or scale and a vernier caliper marked in inches and fractions. This doesn't simplify the problem. It totally avoids it for all shop operations except those requiring power tools that have built-in Metric scales.

If this is not practical, I suggest that before tedious measurement conversion, the woodworker first examine the project drawings and dimensions. Some puzzles, such as *Bi-Burr*, have very few dimensions. A one-inch dimension can be converted to 25.4 mm easily enough and one-half inch translates to 12.7 mm. But it is probably far simpler to slightly alter the basic dimensions to 24 mm and 12 mm, eliminating the need to carry the clumsy decimals and facilitating measurement throughout the project. And remember, with projects like *Bi-Burr*, in the end the fit of the mating parts counts far more than the actual dimensions.

For other projects, such as *Aha Box*, woodworkers who must work in the Metric system will have to convert all of the dimensions. Study the illustrations and determine which dimensions need to be converted precisely and which do not require carrying those messy decimal places, which dimensions affect fit and function and which are less fussy. Use the simple equivalence, 1 in. = 25.4 mm, or refer to the following table. Seldom, if ever, will it be necessary to bother with any conversion closer than 0.05 mm, about 0.002 in.

Inches	mm*	inches	mm*	inches	mm
$\frac{1}{64}$	0.40	$\frac{33}{64}$	13.10	1	25.4
$\frac{1}{32}$	0.79	$\frac{17}{32}$	13.49	2	50.8
$\frac{3}{64}$	1.19	$\frac{35}{64}$	13.89	3	76.2
$\frac{1}{16}$	1.59	$\frac{9}{16}$	14.29	4	101.6
$\frac{5}{64}$	1.98	$\frac{37}{64}$	14.68	5	127.0
$\frac{3}{32}$	2.38	$\frac{19}{32}$	15.08	6	152.4
$\frac{7}{64}$	2.78	$\frac{39}{64}$	15.48	7	177.8
$\frac{1}{8}$	3.18	$\frac{5}{8}$	15.88	8	203.2
$\frac{9}{64}$	3.57	$\frac{41}{64}$	16.27	9	228.6
$\frac{5}{32}$	3.97	$\frac{21}{32}$	16.67	10	254.0
$\frac{11}{64}$	4.37	$\frac{43}{64}$	17.07	11	279.4
$\frac{3}{16}$	4.76	$\frac{11}{16}$	17.46	12	304.8
$\frac{13}{64}$	5.16	$\frac{45}{64}$	17.86	13	330.2
$\frac{7}{32}$	5.56	$\frac{23}{32}$	18.26	14	355.6
$\frac{15}{64}$	5.95	$\frac{47}{64}$	18.65	15	381.0
$\frac{1}{4}$	6.35	$\frac{3}{4}$	19.05	16	406.4
$\frac{17}{64}$	6.75	$\frac{49}{64}$	19.45	17	431.8
$\frac{9}{32}$	7.14	$\frac{25}{32}$	19.84	18	457.2
$\frac{19}{64}$	7.54	$\frac{51}{64}$	20.24	19	482.6
$\frac{5}{16}$	7.94	$\frac{13}{16}$	20.64	20	508.0
$\frac{21}{64}$	8.33	$\frac{53}{64}$	21.03	21	533.4
$\frac{11}{32}$	8.73	$\frac{27}{32}$	21.43	22	558.8
$\frac{23}{64}$	9.13	$\frac{55}{64}$	21.83	23	584.2
$\frac{3}{8}$	9.53	$\frac{7}{8}$	22.23	24	609.6
$\frac{25}{64}$	9.92	$\frac{57}{64}$	22.62	25	635.0
$\frac{13}{32}$	10.32	$\frac{29}{32}$	23.02	26	660.4
$\frac{27}{64}$	10.72	$\frac{59}{64}$	23.42	27	685.8
$\frac{7}{16}$	11.11	$\frac{15}{16}$	23.81	28	711.2
$\frac{29}{64}$	11.51	$\frac{61}{64}$	24.21	29	736.6
$\frac{15}{32}$	11.91	$\frac{31}{32}$	24.61	30	762.0
$\frac{31}{64}$	12.30	$\frac{63}{64}$	25.00	31	787.4
$\frac{1}{2}$	12.70	1 inch	25.40	32	812.8

Using this table, $2\frac{11}{32}$ in., for example, would convert to 50.8 + 8.73 = 59.53 mm

*Rounded to the nearest 0.01 mm

Allan J. Boardman

Allan Boardman has been interested in and involved with both puzzles and woodworking nearly all of his life. Some of his earliest memories, dating back to his preschool days, are of making models and toys in his basement workshop in New Jersey. His father would often take him to New York City to visit a puzzle shop in Rockefeller Center to find new and challenging puzzles. These two interests began to coalesce and mature during his years at MIT when he should have been studying instead of spending time in the campus wood shop.

After receiving his degree in Aeronautical Engineering in 1955, Boardman moved to Southern California to begin his professional career, searching for a position in the nascent space business. After a few journeyman years at North American Aviation (now Rockwell), and Ramo-Wooldridge, he settled at the Aerospace Corporation and rose to the position of Group Vice President for Engineering and Technology before retiring in 1996. During those years, he married, built a home in the San Fernando Valley, and raised three children with his wife Lina. For a number of years, most of his workshop time was devoted to household projects and making furniture, but his passion for puzzles was always roiling just beneath the surface.

During the 1970s, the vast number of closet woodworkers began to connect with each other, partly because of the appearance of *Fine Woodworking*, a magazine dedicated to quality methods, projects, and sources of supply for the hobbyist and small business woodworker. During the same period, Boardman met with a small band of mechanical puzzle enthusiasts in the United States, Japan, and Europe who formed the nucleus of a truly international group, now numbering more than 500 individuals, who communicate by way of the Internet and meet annually to share new puzzle ideas.

In addition to making wooden puzzles, Boardman has written numerous articles for woodworking magazines such as *Fine Woodworking* and *The American Woodworker* on woodworking techniques and puzzle projects. He has taught classes and lectured on these subjects for the past 30 years at woodworking stores, hobby clubs, and trade shows. Many of his current projects are small wooden mechanical puzzles (he calls himself a microxylometagrobologist), some of which can be seen on the Internet at *johnrausch. com.*

More great woodworking books from Linden Publishing

Unique Wood Lamination Projects
by Jerry Syfert
8.5 x 11. 88 pages. Paper.
$19.95/Canada $26.95.
ISBN: 0941936880

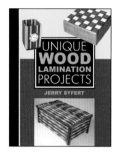

Chairmaking and Design
by Jeff Miller.
8 x 10. 199pp. Paper.
$22.95/Canada $28.95.
ISBN: 1933502061

All Screwed Up
by John Berkeley.
8 x 11.5. 120pp. Paper.
$24.95/Canada $33.95
ISBN: 0941936937

Greene & Greene Design Elements for the Workshop
by Darrell Peart.
8.5 x 11. 128pp. Paper.
$24.95/Canada $37.95 .
ISBN: 0941936961

Making Working Wooden Locks by Tim Detweiler
8.5 x 11. 96 pages. Paper.
$21.95/Canada $32.95.
ISBN: 0941936600

Art of Segmented Woodturning
by Malcolm Tibbetts.
8.5 x 11. 184pp. Paper.
$25.95/Canada $38.95
ISBN: 0941936864

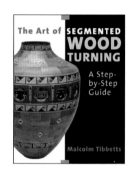

New Wood Puzzle Designs
by James Follette M.D.
8.5 x 11. 96 pages. Paper.
$21.95/Canada $32.95.
ISBN: 0941936570

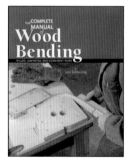

The Complete Manual of Wood Bending
by Lon Schleining
8.5 x 11. 190 pages. Paper.
$25.95/Canada $34.95
ISBN: 0941936546

Traditional Wooden Toys
by Cyril Hobbins.
8 x 10. 180pp. Paper.
$24.95/Canada $31.95. ISBN:
193350210x

Sharpening with Waterstones
by Ian Kirby
6 x 9. 112 pages. Paper.
$14.95/Canada $22.95
ISBN: 0964399938

World Woods in Color
by William Lincoln
7 x 10. 320 pages. Cloth.
$59.95/Canada $81.95.
ISBN: 0941936201

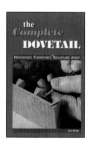

The Complete Dovetail
by Ian Kirby
6 x 9. 152 pages. Paper. $14.95/
Canada $22.95.
ISBN: 0941936678

28. The space required for a parking lot to accommodate 325 cars, parked at 90 degrees, is approximately

A. 1.5 acres   C. 3.0 acres

B. 2.5 acres   D. 6.0 acres

29. The most effective way to diminish the effects of urban noise is by

A. increasing the distance between the noise source and the receiver.

B. providing a physical barrier of plant material.

C. creating water movement, such as a fountain.

D. eliminating private vehicular traffic.

30. Air which is moving at a speed of 100 feet per minute may be described as

A. pleasant.   C. unnoticeable.

B. drafty.   D. unbearable.

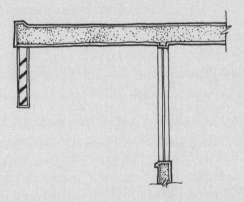

31. The shading device illustrated in the section above would be most effective to

A. reduce the solar radiation on a south elevation.

B. reduce the solar radiation at low sun angles.

C. permit maximum sun control with air circulation.

D. permit maximum sun control with optimum view.

32. Bulb tees are generally used

A. in foundation work involving caissons.

B. in underpinning as a form of temporary support.

C. in gypsum concrete roof deck construction.

D. as water stops in below-grade concreting.

33. The planning phase of a sustainably designed architectural project should include which of the following elements?

I.   Native landscaping that is aesthetically pleasing and functional

II.   Designing structures in the floodplain that can resist the forces of flood waters

III.   Consideration of sun orientation, topographic relief, and the scale of adjacent buildings

IV.   Locating projects within existing neighborhoods that are adjacent to public transportation

A. I and II

B. I and III

C. I, III, and IV

D. All of the above

34. Sustainably designed architecture requires attention to which of the following building elements?

I.   Solar shading devices

II.   Urban heat island effect

III.   Increased parking

IV.   Fenestration and glazing

A. I, II, and IV

B. I and IV

C. I and II

D. All of the above

35. A new building is being constructed adjacent to an existing building whose footings are shallower than those planned for the new structure. The foundation for the new building should be constructed

A. in the usual way, as the existing building's footings will be minimally disrupted.

B. to the same depth as the footings in the existing building.

C. after the footings of the existing building have been extended down to the depth of the footings of the proposed building.

D. in two steps: first on the three non-adjacent sides and then on the remaining side.

The examination answers and explanations will be found on the following pages.

Do not look at the answers until you have completed the exam.

1. **D** Soil test borings are drilled in order to investigate the subsoil conditions existing on a particular site. When subsurface conditions are relatively uniform, borings may be spaced further apart. Conversely, more borings are required as the shape of the ground floor plan becomes more complex, and as the floor area increases in size. The number of borings, however, is unaffected by the depth of firm strata. Regardless of where these strata are encountered, borings should extend at least 20 feet into such strata, if possible, unless the material cannot be penetrated, such as rock.

2. **D** Using a tree windbreak or masonry barrier will be only moderately successful in blocking uncomfortable winds, since the greatest wind force flows down the face of the building and creates a high-velocity vortex at ground level. The best solution, if possible, is to locate the entrance plaza on the leeward, rather than the windward, side.

3. **C** Vandalism, which is the willful destruction of property, may be controlled to somedegree with the use of floodlighting, guard dogs, or burglar alarms. However, the results of vandalism can be reduced by using impact-resistant materials or those that are difficult to damage and easy to repair or clean.

4. **B** An aquifer is the permeable underground rock or earth through which water flows. Definition C refers to the ground water table, while definitions A and D are irrelevant.

5. **A** Materials with high heat-storage values (thermal inertia) are most appropriately used in areas with high daily temperature variations, such as Phoenix. In such hot and arid locations, concrete or masonry walls store heat during the day and later release this heat when the temperature drops, which tends to balance the extremes of day and night. There is little benefit to using high heat-storage materials in hot and humid areas with little temperature variation, such as the other cities listed.

6. **B** Pile foundations are used where the soil strata beneath a structure are incapable of supporting the imposed building loads using conventional spread footings. They may be constructed from timber, concrete, or steel (III), unlike conventional footings that are invariably made of concrete. Compared to conventional spread footings, pile foundations are generally more costly (I), but they do not outlast spread footings (II). Pile foundations do not normally support greater building loads (IV), nor are they generally constructed more quickly (V).

7. **D** Deed restrictions are clauses in a deed that place conditions, limitations, or restrictions on the use of property. Private developers often impose such restrictions on buyers for the purpose of maintaining the consistency or integrity of a development. All of the other terms listed refer to restrictions imposed by, or approvals granted by, local governmental agencies.

8. **D** Zoning ordinances are laws established by local governmental agencies to regulate and control land use for the general welfare of people living or working in the area. They may achieve any of the results listed, with the exception of diminished fire danger, which is more properly the concern of building codes.

9. **B** According to the ANSI Standards, handicapped parking spaces must be at least 8'-0" wide and have an adjacent access aisle that is a minimum of 5'-0"

wide. In addition, the access aisle must be part of a 3'-0" wide access route leading to the building entrance.

10. **A** A catchment area, also known as a market area or trade area, is the tributary area from which a facility derives its user population. Depending on the type and size of the shopping center, the catchment area fluctuates in size on the basis of travel time and convenience in reaching the facility.

11. **C** A sun chart shows the path of the sun, by means of altitude (I) and azimuth (II), usually on the 21st day of each month, from sunrise (V) to sunset. The amount of sunshine (III) is based on the cloudiness at a particular location, and this cannot be determined from a sun chart. Finally, degree days (IV) is a unit used to estimate the heating requirements of a building at a particular locality, and it too is unobtainable from a sun chart.

12. **C** The purpose of drainage systems is to collect, conduct, and dispose of excess rain water. Complex drainage systems are required when any of these three purposes cannot be accomplished in a natural way. Paving or grading the hillside might help collect and conduct water, but neither would dispose of the water. Therefore, one would be better off to provide a thick ground cover, which would slow down the rate of runoff. This would allow greater water absorption and percolation into the soil, as well as reduce erosion. Finally, an earth berm at the toe of the slope would do little more than dam or divert the surface flow, again without solving the problem of water disposal.

13. **C** Large housing projects devote much of their total cost to site work, such as grading, road construction, utility layouts, etc. Therefore, the most efficient organizational form would be a centralized or compact

arrangement that would group these costly elements in the smallest possible area.

14. **A** Suburban shopping malls are generally planned with *anchor tenants*, which are major department stores located at both ends of a shopping street. The street may be crossed by secondary paths perpendicular to the primary axis. Although this arrangement is similar to a linear pattern, axial patterns are distinguished by their orientation to fixed objects at the ends, while linear patterns are more open-ended.

15. **B** The development of classical Rome was based on the gradual accumulation of self-contained building complexes. Each served a distinct activity and interrelated with its neighbors. Thus, Rome achieved a rational order through a precinctual arrangement of separate, balanced components. Precinctual patterns allow growth in any direction and are generally flexible, compact, and efficient.

16. **D** Deed restrictions, zoning ordinances, and easements all represent legal restrictions that prescribe and enforce limitations on the use of property. Environmental impact statements (EIS), however, provide a basis for regulatory agencies to review a project's effect on the environment. Impact statements do not determine a project's approval; they are simply a means of studying a project's potential negative impact and possible alternatives.

17. **A** The amount of solar radiation received by a site is determined by its latitude (distance from the equator) and its slope. The closer the rays are to being perpendicular to the ground surface, the greater the amount of solar radiation. Wind patterns and longitude do not affect solar radiation.

18. A A clue to the topographic profile can be found by proceeding from either end of the section line in order to determine whether the land rises or falls. Since the section cut line parallels the contours on the right, we know that the right side of the section must be represented by a level line, and therefore we can immediately rule out choices B and C. As we follow the section cut line from right to left, it is apparent that the land rises steadily. Thus, there is little doubt that section A is the correct topographic profile.

19. A Building orientation is determined largely by external influences, such as climate, noise, and views. Orientation plays a major role in sheltering outdoor spaces from strong winds, in shielding spaces from airborne noise sources, and in receiving solar energy. The building's foundation system, however, is unrelated to orientation on the site.

20. D The existing slope of 5 in 20 translates to a 25 percent grade ($5 \div 20 \times 100 = 25\%$), which is far too steep for parking cars. Regrading the site is necessary, and the finish grade should not exceed 0.5 in 10, which represents a 5 percent grade. Paved driveways, however, may be as steep as 10 percent.

21. A Organic soil, such as peat, is elastic, weak, and has little cohesion. For these reasons, it is normally removed and replaced in areas to be developed. Since loose silt may be compacted or, in some cases, used as is, a site with organic soil would be more costly to develop.

22. D An architect is obliged to make a reasonable attempt to solve a client's problem. The fact that a site slopes and has some loose fill is not reason enough to reject the site. Sloping areas with loose fill may be leveled and used for outdoor play,

or they may inspire a more imaginative plan.

23. B Choice I would encourage automobile usage, and is therefore an incorrect choice. The other three choices would all help to reduce automobile usage to some extent. Monthly market-rate parking (II) would be partly effective since only building occupants (or occupants of other buildings nearby) would use the parking. III would be most effective, although such a system is not in common use. IV is practical and in common use, but the incentive rates might be eliminated if the owner of the building were not making a sufficient profit, rendering its continued usage uncertain.

24. B Poor drainage is indicated by a high water table (III), since relatively little water could seep into the ground before it would reach a point of saturation. A relatively flat site (IV) would also drain poorly, since the water would tend to pond, rather than flow. Finally, with no storm drainage system (V), all surface water would drain haphazardly, rather than be conducted effectively away from the site. The other two choices would actually indicate good drainage. Dense groundcover (I) would impede the water flow and allow the earth to absorb the moisture, and a flowing stream (II) would act as an efficient surface drainage system.

25. A As the elevation increases, the temperature decreases by about one degree for every 300 feet or so, because the thinner air of higher altitudes is unable to hold as much heat. Therefore, the mountain resort would always be cooler than a town located 3,000 feet below it.

26. A In questions such as this, one must not confuse percentage of slope with degree of slope. For example, a 10 percent slope, which means a vertical rise of 1 foot for a horizontal length of 10 feet, corresponds to a slope of about 6 degrees. With that in mind, the following grades are generally accepted standards. Storm drains slope between 0.3 percent and 1 percent, pedestrian walks should not exceed a slope of 10 percent or up to 15 percent for very short ramps, and planted banks should not exceed a slope of 50 percent. The maximum slope of unretained earth cuts varies from 50 percent to 100 percent, depending on the type of soil. Finally, drainage ditches vary in slope from a minimum of 2 percent to a maximum of 10 percent.

27. **D** The microclimate of an area is affected by its ability to absorb radiant energy. A planted area will absorb and store the heat it receives during the day and release this same heat when the temperature drops. Structures and paving, on the other hand, produce extremes of heat and cold in direct relation to the sun during the day and the cold at night. The planted area, therefore, tends to stabilize the microclimate. Plants also increase the area for transpiration, thereby making it more likely that rainfall will increase, not decrease. Both plants and structures affect air movement, and in this respect, there is little difference between the two. Although plants may purify the air around them, the small amounts of smoke and dust that they trap are relatively insignificant.

28. **C** To solve this problem, one must know the number of square feet to allow per car for parking areas, as well as the number of square feet in an acre. Using the usual estimate of 400 square feet per car, the total area required is $400 \times 325 = 130,000$ square feet. If this total is divided by the number of square feet in an acre (43,560), the result is $130,000 \div 43,560 = 2.98$, which is closest to the correct answer of 3.0 acres.

29. **A** Noise pollution is a fact of life in every major city, and its control continues to be a source of concern. Each of the choices listed would help reduce the effects of urban noise to some extent. The most effective of these, however, is to increase the distance between the noise source and receiver, since sound decreases as the square of the distance from a point source. Plant material helps to disperse sound, and moving water masks sound. Finally, even if it were possible to eliminate private cars (which is unlikely), there would still be noise from buses, trucks, and other vehicles.

30. **A** Air movement is only one factor that determines the degree of comfort. Other factors are temperature, humidity, and radiation. At an average temperature of 75 degrees with about 30 percent relative humidity, air moving at 100 fpm is quite pleasant. At less than 50 fpm, air is generally unnoticeable; while at 250 fpm or more, breezes can be drafty and annoying.

31. **B** The shading device shown offers effective protection from low sun angles, where it is important to place an obstruction between the sun and glass. This protection is most effective on the east and west, but not as useful on a south elevation, where the sun is at its highest angle. Although the device shown would permit sun control and air circulation, it would certainly not be the maximum amount possible. Nor would it provide the optimum view, unless it were located several stories high and the predominant view were downward.

32. **C** Bulb tees are used in gypsum concrete construction as structural sub-purlins. The bulb tees are fastened to the primary

framing and provide support for the form boards that receive the gypsum concrete. They also anchor the deck against uplift forces, restrict deck movement due to temperature changes, and provide lateral bracing for the roof structure. Gypsum concrete roof decks are lightweight, they set rapidly (30 minutes), and when used over gypsum or mineral fiber form boards, they are classified as noncombustible.

33. C Choice I is correct: Designing with native landscaping is preferred to using exotic or imported plant types. Indigenous plants tend to survive longer, use less water, and cost less. Choice II is not correct: Placing any structure in a floodplain, even those that resist floodwater, is not desirable. Placing buildings in a floodplain can increase flooding further downstream. Choice III is also correct: Buildings sensitive to the benefits of solar orientation and passive and active solar gain techniques save energy and are more visually aligned with local climatic conditions. Choice IV is correct as well: In-fill development and proximity to a variety of transportation options are design principles that benefit the inhabitants and their environment.

34. A I is correct: Solar shading, whether from landscaping or architectural elements, can regulate the insulation to increase winter light and reduce warm summer sunlight. II is also correct: Urban heat island effect is the tendency of a building roof to absorb solar radiation during the day and then emit heat radiation during the evening. Roof systems with grass or light colored roofing material reduce the urban heat island effect. III is not correct: Sustainable design encourages approaches that reduce the area allocated to parking. IV is correct: The type, location, and size of building fenestration are a key aspect of architectural design for sustainable projects.

35. C No excavation for the new footings should be started until the footings of the existing building are first extended down to the level of the proposed building's footings. This is accomplished by using temporary supports, such as timber shores or steel needle beams, to carry the weight of the existing building until the new and lower foundation is in place. When the entire weight of the existing wall is transferred to the new section of the foundation, the shoring and underpinning are removed and the foundation for the new building may proceed. The new work is generally performed on all sides simultaneously.

INDEX